SCAMISTAN

HOW INDIA'S CYBERCRIME INDUSTRY SCRIPTS DIGITAL CHAOS

CHHAVI LAMBA

notionpress.com

INDIA · SINGAPORE · MALAYSIA

ISBN
Paperback 979-8-89673-472-7
Hardcase 979-8-89699-391-9

Dedication

To the internet, our wonderful, chaotic enabler.
Without you, there'd be no memes, no cat videos,
and certainly no scam calls from "your bank" at 3 a.m.
You've truly given us everything, including this book
(and a healthy dose of paranoia).

To the scammers of Scamistan,
you've made an industry out of "Hello, Sir/Madam" and inspired a nation to
double-check every email, call, and QR code.
Here's to your creativity, even if it's a bit... misdirected.
Maybe one day you'll consider a career in cybersecurity
instead of stealing savings one OTP at a time.

To the cybersecurity superheroes who fight an endless battle against phishing,
ransomware, and those never-ending "forgot password"
requests. You're basically the Avengers of the digital world
minus the capes, but with way cooler tech.

And to the victims of cybercrime,
who trusted just a little too much and clicked just a little too soon,
this book is for you. Let's laugh, learn, and ensure that the next time someone
says, "You've won a lottery!" you'll reply with the only reasonable response:
"Nice try, buddy."

Contents

Acknowledgment

First off, a big thank you to the internet, because without it, we wouldn't have online shopping, meme culture, or, well, this book. Let's be honest, if the digital world didn't exist, neither would Scamistan. Phishing? Deepfakes? OTP fraud? None of it. Jamtara would still just be that quiet town where nothing much happens except maybe the occasional power cut.

Speaking of Jamtara, a sarcastic round of applause for the scammers who've put it on the map (for all the wrong reasons). Your creativity, while highly illegal, is undeniably impressive. Here's hoping your future career paths veer more toward cybersecurity rather than scamming. Seriously, imagine the impact you'd make patching vulnerabilities instead of creating them.

A heartfelt thanks to the cybersecurity experts who are out there every day battling ransomware, phishing, and deepfakes while the rest of us binge-watch reality TV. Your work may sometimes feel like an endless game of digital whack-a-mole, but trust me, the world needs you more than it needs another season of that dating show.

To the residents of Jamtara and other hotspots like Delhi, Bengaluru, and beyond, those who are just trying to live their lives without becoming part of a cybercrime Netflix documentary, thank you for your patience. It can't be easy explaining to everyone that *not everyone in your town is running a scam.*

And finally, to you, dear reader, whether you're here to laugh at the absurdity of cybercrime or trying to avoid becoming the next "oops, I shared my OTP" victim, thank you for picking up this book. I hope it entertains you, educates you, and leaves you with just the right amount of skepticism for the next "urgent" call you get.

Remember, in the world of Scamistan, the golden rule is: if it sounds too good to be true, it probably comes with a fake QR code. Stay vigilant, stay curious, and stay amused!

Introduction: Welcome to Scamistan

If you've ever gotten a call claiming you've won ₹25 lakh in a lottery you never entered, congratulations, you've just had a brush with Scamistan. It's not a place you'll find on a map, but it exists everywhere: on your phone, in your email inbox, and lurking behind too-good-to-be-true investment schemes. Scamistan is a state of mind or rather, a state of mischief, where cybercriminals thrive, and unsuspecting victims learn the hard way that the only thing faster than a scammer is their internet connection.

In the heart of this digital underworld, India stands as a curious paradox. On one hand, it's a global hub for IT innovation; on the other, it's the unwitting ground zero for some of the most audacious cyber scams. This book isn't just about Jamtara, the infamous phishing capital of India, it's about how an army of resourceful fraudsters turned deception into an industry, one OTP at a time.

"Scam Likely" Isn't Just a Warning Anymore

Gone are the days when scams were limited to stolen wallets or shady pyramid schemes. Today, scams are digitized, industrialized, and globalized. Cybercriminals don't just steal, they script elaborate dramas where you're the star of a tragic comedy. From fake customer support calls ("Sir, we're from your bank. Please share your card details to block a fraud") to deepfake videos of government officials asking for donations, Scamistan has taken scamming to a whole new level.

Why This Book?

This isn't your typical tech manual, dripping with jargon and written in a language only your IT department understands. No, this is a journey into the heart of digital deception, told with humor, sarcasm, and just the right amount of frustration. Whether you're a tech novice or a cybersecurity pro, this book offers something for everyone:

- **For the uninitiated:** You'll learn to spot scams before they spot you.

- **For industry experts:** You'll nod knowingly as we dissect the inner workings of cybercrime syndicates.

- **For everyone else:** You'll laugh, gasp, and maybe even double-check that suspicious email in your inbox.

From Phishing Hooks to Fake Books

Scamistan isn't just about phishing calls or fraudulent websites, it's a complex web of call centers posing as customer support, cryptocurrency platforms promising guaranteed returns, and hackers who can clone your voice better than Siri. Along the way, we'll meet the masterminds (yes, some of them still use Nokia feature phones), the victims (who learned the hard way), and the tech that makes it all possible.

We'll explore how Jamtara became synonymous with phishing, but also how cybercrime expanded to cities like Delhi, Bengaluru, and Mumbai. From burner phones to AI-driven scams, this book unveils the tools, tricks, and tactics of the trade, all while ensuring you don't feel like you're sitting through a cybersecurity seminar.

Why Humor?

Because if we don't laugh at the absurdity of it all, we might just cry. Humor is a survival tool when navigating the madness of modern scams. Let's face it, scammers are clever, resourceful, and occasionally even funny (seriously, who thought up the Nigerian prince scam?). But with the right knowledge and a healthy dose of skepticism, you can beat them at their own game.

So buckle up, keep your wits about you, and remember: the only jackpot you'll win from a random call is the lesson never to answer it in the first place. Welcome to Scamistan, where the first rule is simple: trust no one, especially that email promising you an inheritance from a distant relative you didn't know existed.

Now, let's dive in. Spoiler alert: it's going to be a wild ride.

The Cyber Snare

A message pings, too good, too sweet,

A tempting offer, a promised feat.

Click here, they say, to claim your prize,

But all that's waiting are tangled lies.

Behind the screen, a hidden face,

A faceless foe in digital space.

They prey on trust, on hopes, on fear,

And steal what's held so dear, so near.

A phishing line, a fake request,

A stolen heart, an empty chest.

Bank accounts drained, identities gone,

In this cruel game, there is no dawn.

Yet in the wires, amidst the gloom,

We must be smart, make no room,

For scams that pull us in so deep,

We must not let them make us weep.

Guard your passwords, guard your mind,

In this cyber world, be sure, be kind.

Though the scams will never cease,

With care and thought, you'll find your peace.

Chapter 1

Phishing Genesis:
From Jamtara to a Nationwide Empire

The Birthplace of Phishing: Jamtara

In the early 2000s, Jamtara, a small town in Jharkhand, was just another rural area grappling with unemployment and poverty. By 2010, it had become the phishing capital of India, with over 60% of the nation's cybercrime traced back to this single location (NCRB). What made Jamtara infamous was its ability to turn phone calls into an art form of fraud.

Why Jamtara?

1. **Unemployment and Poverty:** With few legitimate job opportunities, scamming became a way out for the youth.

2. **Connectivity:** Affordable mobile data and cheap smartphones meant that even remote areas could connect to a global audience.

3. **Anonymity:** Using burner phones and fake IDs, scammers could operate with little fear of getting caught.

How It Worked

The modus operandi of early Jamtara scammers was surprisingly simple:

- Call a victim, posing as a bank officer or telecom service provider.

- Create urgency by claiming the victim's account or SIM card would be blocked.

- Ask for sensitive details like OTPs or passwords.

- Siphon off money before the victim even realized what had happened.

How It Worked: A Scam in Action

The early days of Jamtara scams were built on simplicity– call a victim, create panic, and cash in before they could think twice. No complicated hacking, no dark web wizardry, just a cheap phone, a confident voice, and a well-rehearsed script.

Picture this:

It's a regular afternoon. Rajiv, a middle-aged insurance agent, is sitting in his office, sipping tea, and scrolling through WhatsApp forwards about how typing your UPI PIN backward will alert the police (it won't). His phone rings.

"Hello?" he answers, absentmindedly.

"Good afternoon, Sir. I'm calling from XYZ Bank's security department. This is an urgent matter regarding your account," the voice on the other end is polite, professional, and laced with just enough authority to make Rajiv sit up straight.

"What? What happened?"

"Sir, we have detected a suspicious transaction attempt on your account. Someone is trying to withdraw ₹49,999 from your savings account. Can you confirm if this was you?"

Rajiv's heart skips a beat. That's almost fifty grand!

"No! I didn't authorize any transaction!"

"Oh no," the caller continues, voice dropping into a concerned whisper. "Sir, this is serious. It looks like your account has been compromised. We must act fast to block the hacker before they steal all your money."

Rajiv grips his phone tighter. "Oh God! What should I do?"

"Sir, don't panic," the voice assures him, calm as a monk. "I am generating a security OTP to help us block this fraudulent transaction. Please read it out to me as soon as you receive it."

Rajiv hears his phone beep. He checks his messages. A new SMS from his bank:

OTP for transaction: 3-7-9-4-2-1

"It's… 3-7-9-4-2-1," he recites hurriedly.

"Thank you, Sir," the caller says smoothly. "We are now securing your account… Please stay on the line while I finalize this."

Rajiv exhales, relieved. He imagines the scammer, who he still thinks is a bank official furiously typing on a keyboard, battling an imaginary hacker trying to loot his savings.

A few seconds later, the caller speaks again, his tone suddenly cheerful.

"Congratulations, Sir! Your account is now completely secure."

Rajiv sighs in relief. "Thank God. I was so worried."

"You don't have to worry at all, Sir," the scammer replies, barely suppressing a smirk. "In fact, it's so secure now that you won't be able to access it."

A silence hangs in the air.

"What?" Rajiv blinks.

The call disconnects.

Confused, Rajiv opens his banking app. 'Invalid password'. He tries again. 'Incorrect credentials'. His stomach churns as he checks his SMS notifications. A fresh message from his bank stares back at him.

₹49,999 has been debited from your account.

What Just Happened?

Rajiv, like thousands before him, fell for the oldest cyber trick in the book i.e. social engineering. The scammer created fear, urgency, and trust in under three minutes, making Rajiv hand over his One-Time Password (OTP) without even questioning it.

By the time he realized the truth, the fraudster had already withdrawn the money, transferred it through multiple accounts, and disappeared into the ether of digital crime.

This wasn't a rare case. It happened every day, hundreds of times. A simple phone call, a sense of panic, and boom- someone, somewhere, just lost their hard-earned money.

The playbook was always the same: panic the victim, push the urgency, and cash out before they can think.

Welcome to Scamistan, where the calls are fake, but the losses are very, very real.

Data Table: Growth of Cybercrime (2005–2024)

Year	Reported Cybercrime Cases	Estimated Financial Loss (INR Crores)
2005	500	10
2010	15,000	300
2015	50,000	1,000
2020	2,00,000	5,000
2024	5,00,000+	10,000+

Source: National Crime Records Bureau (NCRB)

Case Study: The Infamous Lottery Scam

One of Jamtara's most notorious scams involved a gang that convinced victims they'd won a ₹1 crore lottery. Victims were asked to pay a processing fee of ₹50,000 to claim their prize. One victim, a retired teacher, transferred his life savings of ₹2 lakhs before realizing the lottery didn't exist.

When the gang leader was arrested, he quipped:

"It's not a crime. It's a service, people pay to dream."

The Spread: When Cybercrime Became a Franchise Business

Like any "successful business model," Jamtara's phishing empire didn't just remain a local sensation, it scaled up faster than a viral meme. Soon, other regions across India saw the profitability of deception and decided to hop on the scamwagon. Why let Jamtara have all the fun when cybercrime could be the next big "unicorn startup" (minus the legality, of course)?

With every new "branch" that popped up, cybercrime diversified like a well-funded tech startup, only instead of innovation, it was fueled by burner phones and fake customer service calls. Here's how the "Scamistan Expansion Plan" took shape across the country:

Mewat, Haryana: The Telecom Tricksters

Mewat didn't waste time taking notes from Jamtara's scam syllabus. Sitting conveniently close to Delhi, it became the telecom scam capital, focusing on SIM swapping, fake KYC updates, and mobile wallet fraud.

The formula was simple: convince victims that their mobile service was about to be deactivated, steal their SIM identity, and then empty their accounts. The scam was so effective that in 2023 alone, fraudsters from Mewat managed to siphon off ₹100 crores from unsuspecting victims.

Mewat's scammers knew one thing well, people would rather share their OTP than risk "losing network" on their mobile phones. After all, what's worse than losing money? Losing access to WhatsApp groups filled with bad forwards and unsolicited "Good Morning" messages.

Noida, Uttar Pradesh: The Fake Call Center Capital

If Jamtara was the Bollywood of phishing scams, Noida was its Hollywood counterpart, bigger budget, international reach, and a more "professional" touch. Call centers disguised as tech support sprung up, targeting global victims with the classic, "Sir/Madam, we detected a virus on your computer" scam.

With smooth-talking agents and fake pop-ups that locked people's screens, these fraudsters conned thousands of Americans into paying for non-existent antivirus services. By the time the FBI caught wind of this, Noida's fake call centers had already scammed over $10 million from overseas victims.

Fun fact: Most of these victims weren't even hacked. Their only mistake? Googling "customer support" and calling the first random number they found. Because what could possibly go wrong?

Mumbai, Maharashtra: The Financial Fraud Factory

Mumbai, India's financial hub, naturally upped the game. Why settle for small-time phishing when you could run investment frauds and cryptocurrency scams?

The city saw a rise in fake trading platforms, Ponzi schemes, and dubious investment apps that promised unbelievable returns. People were lured in with high-profit guarantees(because apparently, nobody learned from 2008). By the time they realized their money had disappeared into thin blockchain air, scammers were already sipping cocktails on some undisclosed beach.

Losses from these scams? Over ₹500 crores in 2024 alone The irony? Many victims were finance professionals who probably spent years warning others about bad investments, only to fall for one themselves.

And The Franchise Keeps Growing…

With every new cybercrime hub that popped up, Scamistan expanded like a well-funded startup, except the exit strategy involved police raids instead of IPOs. From fake customer care scams in Rajasthan to credit card frauds in Bengaluru, cybercrime in India evolved into a multi-city, multi-crore enterprise.

The business model was simple:

1. Find a vulnerable population (either locals looking for "easy money" or victims who trust too much).

2. Set up a small operation (burner phones, laptops, and a script tighter than a Bollywood dialogue).

3. Cash out before law enforcement catches up.

With so much innovation in the scam industry, one thing became clear, cybercrime wasn't just a problem anymore. It was a full-fledged ecosystem.

And unless people started hitting "decline" on those scam calls, it was only going to get bigger.

Infographic: The Expansion of Cybercrime

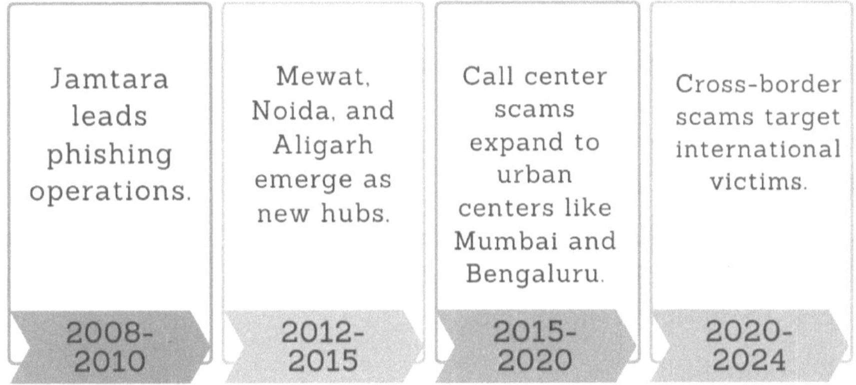

The Call Center Model

By 2015, phishing scams had evolved from small-scale operations into full-blown businesses. Call centers popped up in urban areas, complete with:

- **Recruitment:** Scammers hired young, unemployed individuals and trained them to sound professional.

- **Scripts:** Detailed scripts were created to handle objections and maximize success rates.

- **Incentives:** High-performing "employees" were rewarded with bonuses, luxury goods, and even cars.

Conclusion: A National Epidemic

Jamtara may have been the starting point, but phishing scams are now a national problem. With hotspots emerging in Haryana, Maharashtra, and Uttar Pradesh, the cybercrime empire is thriving. In the next chapter, we'll step inside one of these operations to see how scammers work, think, and innovate.

Chapter 2

Dial M for Mischief:
How Scammers Built a Network Across India

Introduction: A Nationwide Epidemic

What started as a small-town hustle in Jamtara quickly evolved into a nationwide cybercrime empire. By the mid-2010s, phishing wasn't just a scam, it was a scalable business model. No degrees required, no office spaces necessary, and no product to sell, just a phone, a script, and a victim with a little too much trust.

Soon, cybercriminals realized that Jamtara couldn't have all the fun. Other regions saw the sheer profitability of scamming and thought, "Why not us?" The blueprint was simple:

1. Learn the con.

2. Train a team.

3. Expand operations.

4. Rinse, repeat, disappear before law enforcement catches on.

By 2024, phishing had spread like a franchise business, popping up in Mewat, Noida, Mumbai, Kolkata, and even Bengaluru. The criminals collaborated, shared resources, and innovated faster than security agencies could keep up. The result? An underground cyber-industry that thrives on deception.

The Franchise Model: How Scammers Expanded Operations

Step 1: Mentorship & Training – Scam Gurukul

If Jamtara was Scamistan's IIT, then its early fraudsters were the professors of deception. Training sessions weren't held in classrooms but in dimly lit rooms filled with burner phones and whiteboards full of scam scripts.

How It Worked:

- Veteran scammers recruited fresh "students" from villages and urban slums.

- Training modules included:

- How to sound like a bank officer.

- How to make people panic in 30 seconds or less.

- How to fake professionalism with just the right amount of 'Sir/ Madam.'

The best students graduated with burner phones instead of diplomas and were sent to expand operations.

Example: A Classic "Your SIM is Blocked" Scam Call

Victim: Hello?

Scammer: Good evening, Sir. I am calling from Airtel's customer support. This is a security call regarding your SIM card. We have detected unauthorized activity, and your SIM is at risk of being blocked within 24 hours.

Victim (panicking): What? I haven't done anything!

Scammer: Don't worry, Sir. We can fix this right now. I will send a verification OTP, please read it out so we can secure your number.

Victim: Oh, okay… 4-9-3-2-1-0.

Scammer (grinning): Thank you, Sir. Your SIM is now… permanently safe. Well, for me at least.

Victim: Wait, what? Hello? Hello?

What happened? The victim just gave away his OTP for SIM swapping. The scammer cloned his number, took control of his bank OTPs, and drained his account within minutes.

Step 2: Outsourcing Crime – Call Centers, But Make Them Criminal

Just like legitimate companies outsource customer service, scammers outsourced cybercrime. Instead of staying in Jamtara, they moved their call centers to bigger cities like Noida, Mumbai, and Kolkata, where they could blend in among actual BPOs.

Mewat (Haryana): Specializing in telecom scams, fake KYC verifications, and SIM swaps.

Noida (Uttar Pradesh): Fake tech support centers targeting Americans.

Mumbai (Maharashtra): Investment scams and fake crypto platforms.

Bengaluru (Karnataka): Job scams and fake work-from-home offers.

Example: The "Tech Support" Call Center Scam

Victim: Hello, I have an issue with my laptop.

Scammer (fake tech support agent): Sir, your computer has been infected with a very dangerous virus. I need you to download a security tool immediately to fix it.

Victim: Oh no! Okay, what do I do?

Scammer: I will send you a payment link for $199.99 for our premium support. Once you pay, I will remove the virus.

Victim (desperate): Here's my card number…

What happened? The victim just paid for non-existent antivirus software, and the scammers now had access to his bank details.

Step 3: Collaboration & Resource Sharing – Cybercrime's "Open Source" Model

Forget corporate networking, scam syndicates worked together too. Instead of fighting over victims, they shared stolen databases, phishing scripts, and even fake documents.

Databases were exchanged - Millions of stolen emails, phone numbers, and credit card details were passed around.

Fake websites were mass-produced Online banking portals, shopping sites, and loan applications, all designed to trick people into entering sensitive data.

Example: The Fake Loan Scam on WhatsApp

Victim receives a Text message:

"Get an instant loan of ₹5,00,000 with 0% interest for 12 months! No paperwork required. Apply now: [abc.com/loanapplication]"

Victim clicks the link, fills out a form.

Scammer calls the victim:

"Sir, to approve your loan, you must pay a small processing fee of ₹2,999."

Victim pays… and never hears from them again.

What happened? The scammer vanished, and the victim just paid for a loan that never existed.

Data Table: Major Cybercrime Hotspots in India (2015–2024)

Region/City	Key Scams	Estimated Losses (INR Crores)
Jamtara, Jharkhand	OTP phishing, lottery scams	1,200
Mewat, Haryana	SIM swapping, telecom fraud	800
Noida, Uttar Pradesh	Tech support scams, identity theft	2,000
Mumbai, Maharashtra	Cryptocurrency and investment fraud	3,500
Asansol, West Bengal	Fake loans, government schemes	500

Source: National Crime Records Bureau (NCRB)

The Evolution of Phishing Techniques

As cybercrime networks expanded, scammers didn't just stick to basic phishing calls, they innovated, adapted, and upgraded their techniques. What started as simple phone scams demanding OTPs soon evolved into sophisticated frauds powered by SIM swapping, deepfake technology, and AI-driven deception.

This chapter breaks down the most advanced phishing techniques, how they work, and real-life examples of scams that made headlines. These fraudsters weren't just con artists; they were technologists, behavioral psychologists, and expert manipulators who used the latest digital tools to separate people from their money.

1. SIM Swapping: Hijacking Mobile Identities

What It Is:

SIM swapping is a scam where fraudsters take control of a victim's mobile number by tricking telecom providers into issuing a duplicate SIM card. With control over the number, scammers intercept bank OTPs, reset passwords, and take over accounts.

How It Works:

The first step is gathering personal information. Scammers buy stolen identity data from data breaches, dark web markets, or phishing attempts. They might also trick victims into sharing sensitive details by posing as bank representatives or customer support agents.

Once they have enough personal details, the next step is impersonating the victim at a mobile service provider. Armed with fake IDs, they visit a telecom store and request a SIM replacement, claiming the original was lost or damaged. Some scammers also call customer support, using social engineering tactics to convince representatives to approve the request.

As soon as the new SIM is activated, the victim's original SIM card stops working. The scammer now receives all OTPs, verification codes, and SMS notifications linked to the victim's bank accounts and email addresses. Within minutes, they log in, reset passwords, and transfer money out before the victim even realizes their phone has gone silent.

Real-Life Case: Mewat's SIM Swap Heist

In 2021, a cybercrime gang operating in Mewat, Haryana, used SIM swapping to steal over 10 crores from high-profile victims, including CEOs, business tycoons, and celebrities. The fraudsters targeted telecom stores with low-security verification processes, using forged Aadhaar and PAN cards to request duplicate SIMs.

By the time the victims realized their numbers had been hijacked, their accounts had been emptied through rapid transfers and cryptocurrency transactions. During a police raid, authorities recovered 300 fraudulent SIM cards and 2 crores in cash from the scammers' hideout.

2. Fake E-Commerce Websites: Digital Honey Traps

What It Is:

Scammers create fake online stores that mimic real brands and advertise huge discounts on popular products. Once customers make a payment, the items never arrive, and the scam website disappears.

How It Works:

Scammers first create professional-looking websites that copy the logos, images, and design of real e-commerce platforms. They advertise massive discounts on high-demand items like smartphones, laptops, and branded watches, often using Google Ads and Instagram promotions to attract buyers.

Once a victim places an order and pays via UPI or credit card, the scammers either provide a fake tracking number or simply stop responding. By the time the victim realizes something is wrong, the website shuts down, and the fraudsters set up a new one under a different name.

Real-Life Case:

In 2024, Mumbai police busted a fraud network that scammed over 500 crores through fake online stores. The scammers created more than 200 fake websites, advertising discounts on luxury watches, smartphones, and gaming consoles. They used fake celebrity endorsements and social media ads to appear legitimate.

Victims, believing they were buying from genuine brands, made advance payments, but the products never arrived. The fraudsters withdrew the money through multiple fake accounts and shut down the sites within weeks.

3. Cryptocurrency Fraud: The Digital Gold Rush

The cryptocurrency boom was supposed to be a financial revolution. Decentralized, secure, and free from middlemen, crypto was marketed as the great equalizer of wealth, a currency of the future where anyone could become rich overnight. Unfortunately, the only people getting rich were the scammers.

With no regulations, irreversible transactions, and a general lack of public understanding, cryptocurrency quickly became the Wild West of financial fraud. And just like the gold rush of the 1800s, the real winners weren't the people digging for gold, it was the ones selling the shovels. In this case, the shovel-sellers were the scammers running fake crypto trading platforms, promising sky-high returns to unsuspecting investors, only to disappear with their money.

The Illusion of Guaranteed Returns

It always started with an ad usually on social media.

"Want to earn ₹10,000 a day with just ₹500? Start investing in crypto today! No risk, guaranteed profits!"

If that didn't hook people, there was always the next bait: influencers. From flashy Instagram traders claiming to have turned ₹1 lakh into ₹50 lakhs in a month, to paid YouTube "experts" explaining why this was the best investment of the decade, the messaging was always the same, crypto was the easiest way to make money.

And people believed it.

Why wouldn't they? Every influencer was showing off their luxury cars, their fancy vacations, their designer watches, all supposedly funded by crypto investments.

But behind the scenes, it was all an illusion. The influencers were either paid promoters or scammers themselves, using fake profits, rented luxury items, and psychological tricks to convince people to deposit money into fraudulent platforms.

The Trap Closes

The moment someone signed up for one of these platforms, everything seemed real.

The website was well-designed. The trading dashboard looked professional. Numbers changed in real-time. A ₹50,000 investment would show ₹75,000 in profit within days. It was easy to believe you were actually making money.

The platform even had customer support, an AI chatbot that reassured investors when they had doubts.

"Don't worry, Sir. Your profits are growing. Withdrawals are temporarily disabled because of high demand. But keep reinvesting for maximum earnings!"

Some investors, excited by their "profits," doubled or tripled their deposits. They encouraged friends and family to join in.

Then, one morning, the site stopped working.

The login page wouldn't load. Customer support vanished. The Telegram groups went silent. And all the money? Gone.

Real-Life Case: Hyderabad's ₹500 Crore Crypto Mirage

In 2023, a fake crypto trading platform in Hyderabad pulled off one of the largest cryptocurrency scams in India, defrauding over 15,000 investors. The platform promised 200% guaranteed returns, complete with influencer endorsements, live webinars, and an official-looking mobile app.

People poured in their life savings, sold property, and even took loans to invest.

For months, everything looked perfect. Investors saw their balances growing rapidly on the app. Some were even allowed to withdraw small amounts at first, to build trust. But when they tried withdrawing larger sums, they were met with excuses.

"Technical issue. Withdrawals will resume soon."

Then one day, the app vanished.

The website, gone. The customer support numbers, disconnected. The company executives? Nowhere to be found.

By the time the police launched an investigation, the masterminds had converted the ₹500 crores into untraceable cryptocurrency and moved it to international accounts.

4. Deepfake Videos: AI-Driven Scams

What It Is:

Deepfake scams use artificial intelligence to mimic voices and faces, creating highly realistic audio or video messages. Fraudsters use this technology to impersonate executives, government officials, or even family members, tricking victims into transferring money or revealing sensitive data.

How It Works:

Scammers start by collecting voice samples from public videos, phone calls, or leaked recordings. AI software then processes these samples, enabling fraudsters to speak in the victim's voice with near-perfect accuracy.

A fake audio or video message is then created, instructing the target to make an urgent financial transaction. These messages are sent via WhatsApp, email, or even played over a phone call. The victim, hearing what sounds like their boss or relative, follows the instructions and transfers funds, only to realize later that the request was fake.

Real-Life Case: The Deepfake CEO Scam in Bengaluru

In 2023, a finance executive in Bengaluru received a WhatsApp message from his company's CEO, requesting an urgent money transfer of 20 crores for a supposed business deal. The voice sounded exactly like the CEO's, instructing him to wire the funds immediately to a provided account.

Thinking the message was legitimate, the executive approved the transaction. It was only after calling the CEO's personal number later that he discovered the entire request had been fake. By then, the money had already been transferred through multiple shell accounts and withdrawn in cryptocurrency.

Infographic: Cybercrime's Evolution Timeline (2005–2024)

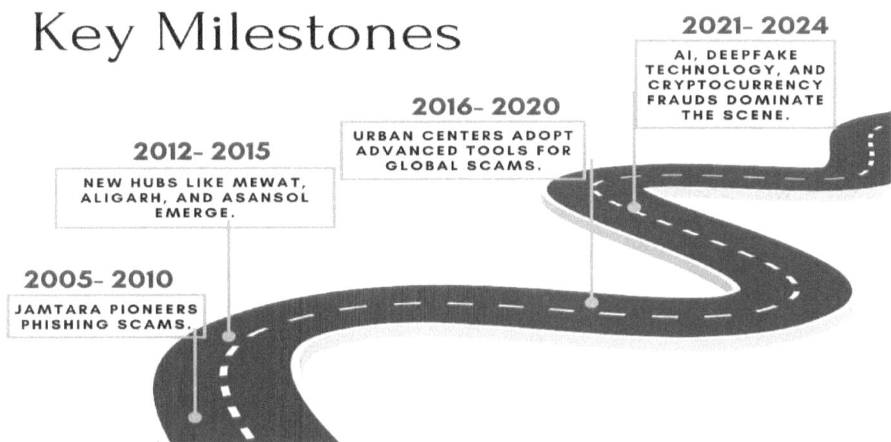

Conclusion: A Well-Oiled Machine of Deception

What started as a small-town hustle in Jamtara has now grown into a sprawling, tech-savvy empire of fraud that operates at a scale no one could have predicted. Cybercrime has evolved beyond simple phishing calls, it has become a self-sustaining industry, complete with recruitment pipelines, training programs, and advanced technological support.

Scammers are no longer lone wolves working in isolation. They operate in organized syndicates, often spanning multiple states and even crossing international borders. Collaboration between cybercrime hubs like Jamtara, Mewat, Noida, and Mumbai ensures that even when one scam operation is shut down, another is already up and running elsewhere.

Authorities scramble to keep up, but cybercriminals innovate faster than law enforcement can respond. With access to stolen databases, AI-powered deepfake tools, and crypto-based money laundering networks, these fraudsters have built an ecosystem where deception isn't just a skill, it's a profession.

The infrastructure of these scams is shockingly efficient. From fake customer support centers and fraudulent investment firms to AI-driven phishing attacks, cybercrime is no longer about just tricking people on a phone call, it's about creating entire digital realities where victims willingly hand over their money.

In the next chapter, we step inside this shadow economy, peeling back the curtain on the daily operations of these scam networks. What does a typical day inside a scam call center look like? How are scammers recruited, trained, and promoted? And most importantly, why is cybercrime growing faster than the efforts to stop it?

The answers might surprise you. And if they don't, well, you're already too familiar with how Scamistan operates.

Chapter 3

Inside the Cyber Call Centers: A Day in the Life of a Scammer

Introduction: Crime as a Profession

The world of phishing scams is often portrayed as a chaotic underworld, but the reality is far more structured. The masterminds behind these operations have adopted the efficiency of corporate models, creating fraudulent call centers that operate like legitimate businesses. With defined roles, targets, and incentives, these scam centers are criminal enterprises in their most organized form.

This chapter takes you inside the operations of India's cybercrime call centers, shedding light on the tools, techniques, and psychology behind their success.

The Daily Grind of a Scam Call Center: Where deception is a 9 to 5 job

Step inside a cybercrime call center, and at first glance, it looks like any other BPO (Business Process Outsourcing) operation. Rows of desks, employees wearing headsets, call scripts taped to their monitors, it all seems like standard corporate hustle. But unlike your typical customer service center, this one doesn't solve problems, it creates them.

The "employees" here aren't tech support specialists or account managers. They are scam artists, trained not to assist but to extract money, personal details, and financial information from unsuspecting victims. Their entire job is built around manipulation, psychological pressure, and deception.

The Shift Begins: Scam O'Clock

A day inside a scam call center starts early, with employees logging into their systems just like regular office workers. But instead of troubleshooting software or handling customer complaints, their targets are already preloaded into a database: phone numbers, email IDs, and personal information leaked from data breaches or bought from underground networks.

Supervisors (often seasoned fraudsters themselves) assign teams based on their expertise. Some focus on bank impersonation scams, while others are responsible for tech support fraud, fake loan offers, or lottery winnings. Like any sales team, they have targets to meet, except here, success is measured not in deals closed, but in money stolen.

A "morning briefing" sets the tone for the day. Strategies are discussed, recent scam successes are celebrated, and new psychological tricks are shared to improve efficiency. Scripts are refined based on what worked the day before, ensuring scammers stay one step ahead of increasingly cautious victims.

The Call Scripts: Manipulation as a Science

The heart of the operation lies in the script. Every scam call follows a carefully crafted narrative, designed to create urgency, panic, or greed whatever it takes to make the victim comply.

For a phishing scam disguised as a bank security alert, the script might go like this:

"Good afternoon, Sir/Madam. This is Rahul from XYZ Bank's fraud department. We've detected an unauthorized transaction attempt on your account for ₹49,999. If this wasn't you, we need to block your card immediately. But before we proceed, we need to verify your identity. Could you please confirm the OTP you just received on your phone?"

The victim, caught off guard and worried about their money, panics and shares the OTP. That's all the scammer needs. Within minutes, they've accessed the account and drained it, often transferring the money to multiple accounts to evade detection.

For a tech support scam, the pitch changes:

"Hello, Sir/Madam. We are calling from Microsoft Support. Your computer has been infected with a severe virus, and hackers may already have

access to your personal data. We can help you remove it immediately, but we need remote access to your device."

Once the victim allows remote access, scammers steal passwords, banking details, and even install ransomware to demand additional payments.

Each call is designed to pressure, confuse, and ultimately extract compliance. And if a victim resists? The scammers have counter-scripts ready, filled with fake legal threats, emotional blackmail, or even fabricated testimonials to keep them on the hook.

Performance Metrics: The More You Steal, The Higher You Rise

Just like any corporate office, scam call centers track employee performance. But here, success isn't measured in customer satisfaction scores, it's measured in "recovery amounts", the total money scammed from victims.

- Those who scam the most people get bonuses and promotions.
- Employees who fail to meet their "revenue targets" face salary deductions or even termination.
- Team leaders motivate staff by celebrating the biggest "wins", cases where victims lost large sums of money without realizing the fraud until it was too late.

To keep morale high, many scam centers operate incentive schemes, rewarding employees with cash bonuses, luxury gifts, or even vacations for their best scam performances.

Lunch Breaks: Scam Stories Over Chai

During breaks, employees gather to share success stories over tea and snacks. Some swap tricks that worked, while others laugh at how easily a particular victim fell for a well-rehearsed lie.

There's a disturbing lack of guilt in these conversations. Most scammers don't see their work as harmful. To them, it's just another hustle, a game of wits where the smart win and the naïve lose. Some even justify their actions by blaming "rich people" or claiming that "banks steal money anyway, so why shouldn't we?"

The Evening Hustle: Last Calls Before the System Resets

As the day winds down, scammers make their final push. This is when they go after elderly victims, knowing that older people are more likely to answer calls in the evening and less likely to verify information.

At the end of the shift, earnings are tallied. The highest-performing scammers are rewarded and recognized. Those who underperformed? They're handed new scripts, given extra training, or in some cases, fired and replaced.

By night, the center may shut down physically, but the online scam operations run 24/7 with automated bots continuing phishing attempts, fake websites harvesting data, and new victims entering the pipeline.

A Never-Ending Cycle

Unlike a legitimate company, scam call centers never stay in one place for long. The moment authorities get close, they shut down, move cities, and set up again under a new name.

Employees who lose their jobs at one call center? They simply find work at another scam operation, often in the same city, with the same scripts, under different management.

This shadow economy of fraud is built to be self-sustaining, constantly evolving, and always one step ahead of law enforcement.

As long as people keep falling for these scams, the call centers will keep running. And for the scammers working there, it's just another job, except the only product they sell is deception.

Let's take a deep dive into this agenda!

Morning Briefing (8:00 AM)

Every day starts with a team huddle, led by the scam center's boss. Targets are assigned, and scripts are rehearsed. The atmosphere is almost motivational, with the boss emphasizing the "importance" of each call.

- **Script Updates:** New lines are introduced to counter potential objections from victims. For example, if victims hesitate to share OTPs, scammers are trained to respond:

  "This OTP is only for verification. It won't be misused."

- **Performance Goals:**

  Scammers are given daily targets, such as extracting ₹50,000 or making a minimum of five successful calls.

Quote from a former scammer:

"It's just like a sales job. The only difference is that we're selling lies."

Morning Blitz (9:00 AM – 1:00 PM)

The first half of the day is dedicated to high-value targets like corporate employees, business owners, and affluent individuals. These victims are seen as "prime" because they often have significant bank balances and less time to scrutinize calls.

- **Focus:** Extracting OTPs, passwords, or direct payments for fake schemes.

- **Psychological Tactics:**

  - *"Your account has been compromised. Act now to secure it."*

  - *"There's a pending refund in your name. Please confirm your details to process it."*

Common Tools Used:

1. **Caller ID Spoofing Apps:** These apps, such as SpoofCard or Fake Call ID, make the scammer's number appear as if it's from a legitimate source.

2. **CRM Software:** Customer Relationship Management tools help scammers keep track of victims, calls, and successful "conversions."

3. **Stolen Databases:** Victim details such as phone numbers, email IDs, and even financial data are sourced from leaked databases available on the dark web.

Lunch Break (1:00 PM – 2:00 PM)

Lunch is often treated as a social hour. Scammers brag about their "earnings" and discuss new techniques to manipulate victims more effectively.

Incentives: Scammers who meet their targets might receive bonuses, such as gift cards, cash rewards, or even motorcycles for top performers.

Case Example:

In one call center busted in Jaipur, employees were promised international vacations if they reached monthly revenue goals.

Afternoon Targeting (2:00 PM – 6:00 PM)

Post-lunch operations shift focus to softer targets, such as homemakers and elderly individuals. These groups are perceived as more trusting and less tech-savvy, making them easier to deceive.

- **Popular Scripts for Homemakers:**
  - *"Your gas subsidy is pending. Please verify your bank account details."*
  - *"We are offering a free insurance policy. Please confirm your Aadhaar number to enroll."*
- **Popular Scripts for Seniors:**
  - *"Your pension account has discrepancies. Share your OTP to fix the issue immediately."*

Wrap-Up and Analysis (6:00 PM – 7:00 PM)

By evening, scammers gather to review their day. Earnings are tallied, and high-performing employees are rewarded with cash bonuses or prizes. Those who fail to meet targets are often berated or given warnings.

Hierarchy:

- **Top Performers:** Receive incentives and promotions within the scam hierarchy.
- **Underperformers:** Are either retrained or replaced.

The Structure of a Scam Call Center: A Corporate Pyramid Of Deception

While most people imagine cybercrime as a messy, underground operation, scam call centers are shockingly organized and professional. They operate like a well-oiled corporate machine, with defined roles, internal hierarchies, and even "performance incentives" except the business model revolves around fraud, and success is measured in stolen money rather than customer satisfaction.

Much like a multi-level marketing scheme, scam call centers have a structured chain of command, with each layer playing a crucial role in ensuring that victims are deceived as efficiently as possible.

The Boss: The Puppet Master

At the top of the pyramid sits the mastermind, the one who never makes a single scam call but takes the biggest cut of the earnings. This individual is the financier, strategist, and ultimate beneficiary of the operation.

- Funds the setup of scam call centers, securing rented office spaces, burner phones, computers, and VoIP software.

- Purchases stolen databases filled with phone numbers, email IDs, and banking details from the dark web or corrupt insiders.

- Pays off local authorities or security personnel to keep the operation running smoothly.

- Ensures that as soon as one call center is compromised, another is ready to replace it.

These masterminds are often career criminals, frequently changing locations, using fake identities, offshore accounts, and cryptocurrency laundering to stay untraceable.

The Team Leaders: The Middle Managers of Fraud

Beneath the boss is the middle management layer, the team leaders who oversee the day-to-day operations. Think of them as the fraudulent version of corporate project managers.

- Manage small groups of recruits (usually 10–20 scammers per team).

- Provide daily motivation, coaching, and script training to improve scam success rates.

- Monitor calls for "quality control", ensuring that scammers use the right psychological tactics to manipulate victims.

- Distribute new scam scripts, adjusting them based on victim responses and recent law enforcement crackdowns.

For top-performing leaders, promotion means moving up the food chain, eventually managing entire regional scam hubs or setting up their own call centers under the boss's network.

The Recruits: The Foot Soldiers of Fraud

At the bottom of the scam pyramid sit the recruits- young, often unemployed individuals lured by promises of easy money. These are the voice actors of deception, the ones actually making the scam calls.

- Many come from small towns and lower-income backgrounds, often tricked into joining by promises of a high salary.

- Others actively seek out the job, knowing full well it's fraudulent but viewing it as just another hustle.

- Paid on a commission basis, meaning their earnings depend on how much money they can extract from victims.

Their training is highly specialized not just in script memorization, but in tone, urgency, and emotional manipulation techniques. Some scammers even undergo mock call sessions where they practice fake conversations until they can scam fluently and convincingly.

The Tech Support Team: The Engineers of Deception

Unlike regular IT professionals, the tech support team in a scam call center isn't there to fix software glitches or update security patches, they are the backbone of fraud, ensuring that the operation runs seamlessly.

- Set up VoIP (Voice over Internet Protocol) systems that allow scammers to disguise their phone numbers to look like legitimate banks, customer care centers, or government agencies.

- Maintain spoofing software that makes it appear as if the call is coming from an official organization.

- Develop fake e-commerce sites, fake bank portals, and investment dashboards that fool victims into believing they are engaging with a real platform.

- Troubleshoot call drop issues and software malfunctions that could disrupt scamming efficiency.

These tech teams are often well-paid, as their skills are essential to scaling up operations. Some are former IT professionals who left legitimate jobs for the higher earnings of cyber fraud.

A Self-Sustaining Machine

Together, these layers form a high-functioning crime syndicate, where everyone has a role to play and the business never stops. Even if a few foot soldiers get caught, the bosses and managers simply hire replacements and relocate.

With money constantly flowing in from victims across the world, these scam centers operate like multi-million dollar enterprises, always staying one step ahead of the authorities.

The question is how do you shut down an industry designed to be unstoppable?

The Tools of the Trade: How Scam Call Centers Stay One Step Ahead

Every industry has its essential tools, chefs have knives, carpenters have saws, and scammers? They have VoIP systems, spoofing apps, and burner phones. While legitimate call centers focus on improving customer experience, scam centers focus on perfecting the art of deception.

Their technology isn't just a convenience, it's their shield against law enforcement and the weapon they use to exploit victims. From hiding their identities to creating fake banking websites, these scammers have an entire arsenal of digital trickery at their disposal.

VoIP Systems: The Invisible Call Center

Before the internet, a scammer's biggest problem was location. If they wanted to con someone in the U.S. while sitting in a small office in Noida or Jamtara, they'd need expensive international calling services.

Enter Voice over Internet Protocol (VoIP) systems, the ultimate scam enabler.

- Allows scammers to make international calls for pennies because nothing kills a good fraud operation like a high phone bill.

- Calls appear to come from official helpline numbers, making it easier to trick victims.

- Unlike traditional phone lines, VoIP calls are harder to trace, giving scammers digital invisibility cloaks.

VoIP transformed cybercrime from small-town phishing scams into a global, billion-dollar fraud industry.

Caller ID Spoofing Apps: When the Bank Isn't Really the Bank

If you've ever received a call from "your bank" asking for your OTP, chances are it wasn't really your bank, it was a scammer using caller ID spoofing software.

These apps allow fraudsters to:

- Make any number appear on the victim's caller ID.

- Impersonate banks, government agencies, or even law enforcement.

- Increase credibility by making it seem like the call is legitimate.

For the victim, it's impossible to tell that the call is fake. The real number of their bank flashes on the screen, and before they know it, they're reading out an OTP that empties their account.

Caller ID spoofing adds an extra layer of psychological manipulation, making scams far more effective.

Burner Phones and SIM Cards: The Disposable Army

Scam call centers never use the same number twice.

Every few days or weeks, scammers switch phones and SIM cards, ensuring that even if a number is flagged or traced, it leads to a dead end.

- Pre-activated SIMs are bought in bulk using fake identities.
- Numbers are rotated frequently to avoid detection by law enforcement.
- If a scam goes viral and victims start reporting the number, scammers ditch the phone and move on.

It's low-cost, high-reward, and nearly impossible to track without breaking through entire telecom networks.

Phishing Kits: Hacking for Dummies

Not all scammers are coding experts. In fact, most don't need to be, because in Scamistan, fraud is pre-packaged for convenience.

Phishing kits are "scams in a box", providing:

- Fake website templates that look exactly like real banking sites.
- Pre-written phishing scripts for scam calls and emails.
- Automated tools that steal login credentials the moment victims enter them.

A scammer doesn't have to build a fake SBI or PayPal login page from scratch, they just buy a phishing kit off the dark web, set it up in minutes, and start stealing credentials at scale.

AI Chatbots: Automating Fraud with Fake Customer Support

Modern scams don't always start with human calls.

Many fraudsters use AI chatbots to initiate conversations with victims, making the scam operation appear professional and legitimate.

- When victims contact fake customer care numbers, they're greeted by a bot that sounds reassuring and efficient.

- The chatbot gathers basic details, filters out skeptical people, and routes serious victims to human scammers for the final deception.

- AI makes operations scalable, allowing scammers to interact with thousands of potential victims simultaneously.

Fraudsters don't just scam, they automate the scam.

Case Study: The Noida Tech Support Scam

In 2023, one of the largest scam call centers in India was busted in Noida. The operation posed as Microsoft tech support, targeting victims in the U.S. and Canada by convincing them that their computers were infected with malware.

The scam worked like this:

1. Scammers used VoIP systems to make calls appear as though they were coming from Microsoft's official helpline.

2. Victims were told that their computers had been hacked or compromised.

3. To "fix" the problem, victims were asked to download remote desktop software, unknowingly giving full access to the scammers.

4. Once inside the computer, fraudsters installed fake malware, then charged victims hundreds or thousands of dollars to "remove" it.

5. Some victims were also tricked into entering their credit card details, which were later used for unauthorized transactions.

By the time authorities raided the call center, the scammers had stolen over ₹80 crores ($10 million) in six months.

A joint operation between the Indian Cybercrime Unit and the FBI led to the arrest of over 50 employees, but the real masterminds remained at large.

The Digital Arms Race: Scammers vs. Law Enforcement

Every time cybersecurity experts find a way to block one scam, cybercriminals invent new tools to stay ahead.

- Banks add two-factor authentication → Scammers use SIM swapping to hijack OTPs.

- People become skeptical of phone calls → Scammers switch to deepfake voice and AI chatbots.

- Authorities crack down on local scam hubs → Operations move online, making them harder to trace.

The battle between scammers and security agencies is a never-ending arms race, with each side trying to out-innovate the other.

For now, the scammers seem to be winning. But as awareness grows and enforcement gets sharper, the question remains, can technology stop what technology created?

Or will Scamistan keep leveling up?

Psychology of a Successful Scam: How Fraudsters Hack The Human Mind.

Cybercrime isn't just about technology, it's about manipulating human behavior. A scam call center doesn't need advanced hacking skills or Hollywood-style cyber intrusions. All they need is a well-rehearsed script, a fake sense of urgency, and a victim on the other end who isn't thinking clearly.

Successful scammers don't break into bank accounts, they convince people to hand over access willingly. It's social engineering at its finest, and it works because fraudsters understand the psychology of decision-making better than most victims do.

How Scammers Exploit Human Nature

1. Creating Urgency: The Art of Panic

Ever noticed how scam calls always start with an emergency? There's always a deadline, a crisis, or a fast-approaching catastrophe.

- *"Your bank account is being hacked RIGHT NOW! You must act immediately!"*

- *"Your phone number will be deactivated in 10 minutes if you don't verify your identity."*

- *"The Income Tax Department has flagged you for fraud! Pay the penalty or face arrest!"*

These tactics short-circuit logical thinking. Victims don't stop to analyze the situation; they react instinctively. When someone is panicking, they don't think about verifying details, they just want to fix the problem before it's too late.

Why It Works: The brain prioritizes immediate threats over rational analysis. Scammers know that as long as they keep victims in panic mode, they can extract information before skepticism kicks in.

2. Building Trust: The Illusion of Legitimacy

Nobody willingly shares their passwords with a random caller. But scammers don't seem like random callers, they sound professional, knowledgeable, and exactly like the customer support representatives victims are used to dealing with.

- They mimic corporate scripts, using technical jargon to sound credible.

- They spoof official phone numbers, making it look like the call is coming from a bank or government office.

- They act polite, patient, and reassuring, until they don't need to be.

By the time the victim realizes something is off, the scammer already has what they need.

Why It Works: Humans are wired to trust perceived authority. If someone sounds like an expert, we tend to believe them.

3. Exploiting Fear: The Threat of Consequences

If urgency doesn't work, fear usually does. Scammers use threats of bank account freezes, police action, legal notices, or even arrest to push victims into compliance.

- *"If you don't provide verification now, your Aadhaar-linked bank account will be locked."*

- *"You have violated RBI regulations. If you don't make a security deposit, legal action will be taken."*

- *"The police have issued a warrant in your name for unpaid taxes. You can avoid this by making an immediate payment."*

Many victims comply out of fear, especially elderly individuals or those unfamiliar with banking procedures. They don't question the legitimacy of the call, they just want to avoid trouble.

Why It Works: Fear triggers a fight-or-flight response, making people more likely to obey authority figures without questioning them.

4. Appealing to Greed: The Fake Jackpot

If panic and fear don't work, greed is always a safe bet. Scammers know that people are more likely to ignore red flags when they think they're getting something for free.

- *"Congratulations! You've won ₹50 lakhs in a lottery! Just pay the processing fee to claim it."*

- *"You're eligible for an exclusive government refund, just verify your details."*

- *"This crypto investment scheme guarantees 500% returns. Don't miss out!"*

Even well-educated individuals fall for investment scams and Ponzi schemes, because the idea of easy money clouds rational judgment.

Why It Works: Humans are drawn to rewards, especially ones that seem easy. If the potential gain looks bigger than the risk, people ignore warning signs.

The Real-World Impact of Scam Call Centers

1. Financial Losses: The Cost of Falling for a Scam

Phishing scams cost Indian individuals and businesses billions every year. According to government data:

- Over ₹10,000 crores were lost to cyber fraud in 2024 alone.

- The average loss per victim in banking scams is over ₹50,000.

- Small businesses suffer huge financial damage, as scammers target employees to extract company funds.

What makes this worse is that many victims never recover their money. Once a scammer receives funds, they quickly move it through multiple accounts, cryptocurrency wallets, and offshore havens, making retrieval nearly impossible.

2. Erosion of Trust: The Call Nobody Believes

The biggest collateral damage from cyber scams is that people stop trusting legitimate services.

- Banks struggle to convince customers that real fraud alerts are not scams.

- Businesses see customers ignore genuine security warnings, assuming they're fake.

- Government agencies have to work twice as hard to verify their authenticity.

As a result, many people ignore actual fraud alerts, because they assume every security call is a scam. This paradox means that real fraud cases often go unresolved, while new scams continue to thrive.

3. Global Reputation: When Scamistan Becomes an International Problem

India's reputation in the global tech industry has taken a major hit due to the rise of cyber scams.

- International fraud victims associate Indian call centers with scams, leading to negative stereotypes.

- Foreign governments pressure India to crack down harder, affecting diplomatic relationships.

- Legitimate Indian IT companies struggle with credibility, as many international clients grow suspicious of outsourcing.

While India is a global hub for legitimate technology services, the dark side of cybercrime continues to tarnish the country's reputation.

Conclusion: Organized Chaos

Inside these scam call centers, fraud isn't seen as a crime, it's seen as a career.

- Employees clock in, run scripts, and track performance metrics, just like any legitimate business.

- Managers train new hires, analyze scam success rates, and improve "conversion strategies."

- Call centers rebrand and relocate as soon as authorities get close, ensuring the operation never stops.

With clear hierarchies, sophisticated tools, and a deep understanding of human psychology, these scam networks are more than just criminal enterprises, they are a well-oiled machine that thrives on deception.

As long as victims continue to trust unverified calls, click suspicious links, and believe in "too-good-to-be-true" offers, these scams will continue.

The only real defense? Awareness. Because in Scamistan, knowledge is the only thing that can save you from becoming the next target.

Chapter 4

Caught in the Net – Victims, Villains, and the Cost of Clicking Wrong

Introduction: Cybercrime's Real Price, More Than Just Money

Let's be honest, nobody thinks they're the kind of person who would fall for a scam.

"I'm too smart for that."
"I'd never give my OTP to a stranger."
"Who even believes these lottery calls anymore?"

Until it happens.

Until you get a call from what sounds exactly like your bank. Until a fake job offer lands in your inbox when you're desperately searching for one. Until someone exploits your fear, greed, or sheer human trust.

Scammers don't just steal money. They steal dignity, trust, and sometimes even hope.

This chapter isn't about statistics or reports. This is about real people: teachers, job seekers, and retirees, who answered the wrong call, clicked the wrong link, or just believed the wrong person at the wrong time.

The Teacher Who Thought He'd Hit the Jackpot

"Congratulations, Sir! You've won ₹1 crore!"

For 62-year-old Rajesh Malhotra, a retired schoolteacher in Kolkata, this call felt like divine intervention.

The caller had an official-sounding voice, mentioned government-approved lottery schemes, and even recited Rajesh's Aadhaar number to prove legitimacy.

"Sir, this is 100% genuine. The only step left is to pay the ₹50,000 processing fee so we can release your winnings."

Rajesh hesitated. The scammer played the clock.

"We only have 48 hours before your winnings expire, sir. You wouldn't want to lose this chance of a lifetime."

Rajesh took the bait.

He transferred the ₹50,000, then waited for the money that never came. A week later, the lottery office's number was disconnected. The jackpot? It existed only in his dreams.

The Psychological Playbook of the Scammer:

- **Greed** – *"Who wouldn't want to be a millionaire overnight?"*

- **Urgency** – *"Act fast, or you'll lose your winnings!"*

- **Authority Bias** – *"I sound professional, so you can trust me."*

The Aftermath:

Rajesh filed a police complaint, but his money was long gone.

"I spent my life teaching kids to be smart. I never thought I'd be the one getting fooled."

He now warns others about these scams but he still feels the sting of betrayal.

The Job Seeker's Nightmare – The Interview That Wasn't Real

When Shivani Arora, a 23-year-old engineering graduate, received an offer letter from a top multinational tech firm, she thought she had finally made it.

- The email looked real.

- The HR executive sounded professional.

- The Zoom interview felt legitimate.

"Congratulations, Shivani! You're hired! We just need a small ₹25,000 training deposit, which will be refunded after six months."

Excited, she sent the money.

The next day, the website was gone.

The HR contact? Vanished.

The company? Never existed.

She had been hired by thin air.

How Scammers Made the Fake Job Seem Real:

- **Phishing Emails** – A domain that looked *almost* like the real company's.
- **Fake Video Interviews** – Conducted over Zoom to build credibility.
- **Cloned Websites** – A near-perfect replica of a real firm's hiring page.

The Impact:

"It wasn't just the money, it was the humiliation. I told my family I had a job. How do you explain to them that you got scammed instead?"

The Pensioner Who Lost Everything in a Five-Minute Call

In 2024, Sushila Devi, a 70-year-old widow from Jaipur, received a call from her "bank manager."

"Madam, there's a serious discrepancy in your pension account. If you don't act now, your monthly pension may be stopped."

She panicked.

"Just share your account details and OTP, and we'll resolve the issue."

She complied.

Within minutes, ₹1.5 lakhs was gone, her entire savings.

When she rushed to her bank, the real manager shook his head. *"We never called you."*

Why Elderly Victims Are Easy Targets:

- **Lack of Tech Awareness** – Many struggle with digital banking.
- **Dependence on Savings** – Scammers know they have pension accounts.
- **Fear and Compliance** – Seniors are less likely to question authority.

Sushila was left with **nothing.**

Who Falls for Scams And Why?

Scammers don't pick victims randomly. They target psychological weak points with precision.

Most Common Victims:

- **Seniors (50+)** – 40% of phishing victims are elderly.
- **Job Seekers (18-30)** – Prone to employment and investment fraud.
- **Homemakers** – Frequently targeted for fake insurance and subsidy scams.

Most Common Psychological Triggers:

- **Urgency** – "Act now or face consequences!"
- **Greed** – "You've won something valuable!"
- **Fear** – "You'll lose money if you don't comply!"
- **Authority Bias** – "I sound professional, so trust me!"

The Ripple Effects of Cybercrime

Cyber scams don't just steal money. They shatter confidence, trust, and peace of mind.

Emotional Trauma:

Victims experience shame, guilt, and anxiety. Many never report the crime, fearing judgment.

Broken Trust:

Legitimate institutions struggle because people stop trusting real calls.

Financial Ruin:

For many victims, the money lost is everything they had.

Quote by Psychologist, Dr. Meera Kapoor:

"The emotional scars last longer than the financial loss. Victims feel violated."

Fighting Back: What Victims Can Do

If you fall for a scam, don't panic, take action.

1. Report the Crime – File a complaint on www.cybercrime.gov.in.

2. Notify Your Bank – They might be able to freeze or recover some funds.

3. Seek Support – Counseling or victim support groups help deal with emotional trauma.

4. Spread Awareness – The more people know, the fewer victims there will be.

Turning the Tables – The Victim Who Outsmarted the Scammers

In 2023, Karan Mehta, a 28-year-old from Mumbai, received a phishing call.

Instead of panicking, he played along.

He pretended to comply but alerted his bank and the police.

Within 48 hours, the scammers were tracked and arrested.

Quote from Karan:

"They thought they had me. I had them instead."

Scammers Are Smart. You Just Have to Be Smarter.

Cybercrime works because scammers understand human nature better than most people do.

The only way to fight back?

Stay skeptical. Stay informed. And never trust anyone who tells you you've won something you never entered.

Data Table: Cybercrime Victims in India (2015–2024)

Year	Reported Victims	Financial Losses (INR Crores)
2015	50,000	1,200
2018	1,50,000	3,000
2022	3,00,000	6,500
2024	5,00,000+	10,000+

Conclusion: Lessons from the Victims: A Masterclass in Digital Caution

If there's one thing these stories teach us, it's this, scammers don't steal money; they steal trust. They manipulate human emotions, weaponize urgency, and create illusions so convincing that even the most cautious individuals fall for them.

Cybercrime isn't just about hacking computers, it's about hacking minds.

Each victim's story is a cautionary tale, a reminder that vigilance isn't optional in the digital age, it's a necessity.

- If a deal sounds too good to be true, it is.
- If a caller creates panic, take a breath before you act.
- If someone asks for personal information over the phone, hang up and verify.
- And if a bank, lottery, or government official needs an upfront payment for anything, congratulations, you've just met a scammer.

By sharing these stories, the goal isn't just to highlight the damage but to prevent the next victim from making the same mistakes. The best way to shut down cybercrime isn't just law enforcement, it's public awareness and skepticism.

Because in a world where scammers get smarter every day, the only way to stay ahead is to be smarter than the scam.

Chapter 5

The Scam Economy: Following the Money Trail

Introduction: Where Does the Money Go?

When you hear about a cyber scam, you probably imagine a fraudster draining someone's bank account, then immediately splurging on a fancy car, a gold chain, and a weekend getaway in Goa. And while that's not entirely wrong, the real money trail is far more sophisticated, global, and deeply entrenched in organized crime.

Cybercriminals aren't just tech-savvy tricksters, they're financial masterminds running an economy of fraud. The stolen money doesn't just disappear into the night; it flows through a carefully planned pipeline of laundering, reinvestment, and expansion.

So, where does all that scammed money go? Does it end up in a scammer's Swiss bank account? Is it buying them a beachside villa? Or is it fueling an even bigger criminal empire?

Let's follow the trail and see how the dirty money moves.

The Scam Economy: A Financial Frankenstein

The cyber fraud industry runs like a well-funded startup, with every rupee extracted from victims being carefully reinvested to maximize profits and minimize risks.

Here's how the money moves:

1. Extraction: Stealing the Cash

Before scammers can enjoy their earnings, they have to steal it first.

- Fake e-commerce websites trick people into making payments for products that don't exist.

- Investment frauds lure victims into depositing money with promises of high returns.
- Phishing calls convince victims to send money through UPI, credit cards, or wire transfers.

Once the money leaves the victim's hands, it doesn't just sit in one account, it gets scrambled faster than an egg in a five-star hotel kitchen.

2. Redistribution: The Digital Laundromat

If scammers kept the stolen money in one place, law enforcement would shut them down in minutes. So, instead, they move it through multiple layers, making it harder to track.

- Cryptocurrency Conversions – Money is converted into Bitcoin or Ethereum, because blockchain transactions are harder to trace.
- UPI Wallets & Digital Accounts – Scammers spread funds across multiple small wallets to avoid detection.
- Money Mules – Regular people (often unsuspecting) receive stolen funds and withdraw them for the scammers.

Think of it like money playing musical chairs, except nobody wants to be the last one holding the bag.

How Scammers Use Technology to Stay Undetectable

1. Cryptocurrency: The Digital Laundromat

Once upon a time, criminals laundered money through fake construction projects and shady offshore accounts. But today's fraudsters? They use crypto.

Why? Because:

- Cryptocurrency transactions are fast, anonymous, and borderless.
- Scammers use "mixers" to scramble transaction histories, making stolen money nearly untraceable.

- They cash out in small amounts, so no red flags are raised.

Real-Life Case: The Hyderabad Bitcoin Laundering Operation

In 2023, a scam ring in Hyderabad laundered ₹300 crores through Bitcoin transactions. Investigators later traced several wallets linked to international criminal networks.

2. Digital Wallets: The Perfect Smokescreen

E-wallets like Paytm, Google Pay, and PhonePe are a scammer's dream.

- They allow instant transactions with minimal scrutiny.

- Fraudsters open multiple accounts using fake KYC details.

- Money is moved in small transactions (usually under ₹20,000) to avoid detection.

Real-Life Case: The ₹50 Crore Digital Wallet Scam in Delhi

In 2022, a network of scammers used over 1,000 digital wallets to launder money from fake investment scams. Each transaction was small enough to stay under banking radar systems, allowing the fraudsters to siphon off ₹50 crores before authorities caught on.

3. Money Mules: The Human ATMs

Scammers don't want money traced back to their accounts, so they use "money mules", people who unknowingly transfer stolen money on their behalf.

- Here's how it works:

1. Scammers send money to a random person's bank account.

2. The mule is told to withdraw the money and pass it on.

3. The mule gets a small cut, while the scammer remains anonymous.

Real-Life Case: The Kolkata Money Mule Network

In 2021, Kolkata police busted a network of over 500 money mules who were withdrawing stolen cyber fraud money for a scam syndicate. Each mule was paid ₹500 per withdrawal, and the operation laundered over ₹200 crores.

How Scammers Spend Their Ill-Gotten Gains

What happens when cybercriminals finally cash out their stolen money? They don't just stash it under their mattresses, they spend it, and spend it big.

Luxury Purchases – "Phishing Trophies"

- Expensive SUVs, gold chains, designer clothes.
- In Jamtara, owning a fancy car is a status symbol among scammers.

Real Estate – Hiding the Money in Property

- Stolen funds are used to buy properties under fake names.
- Shell companies help launder money through real estate investments.

Bribery – Greasing the Wheels

- Some scammers pay off local officials to avoid scrutiny.
- Corrupt cops tip off scam centers before a raid happens.

Quote from an Investigator:

"These criminals run their operations like well-funded startups. They reinvest, expand, and scale fraud like it's a business model."

Real-Life Case: When Scams Funded Terrorism

In 2022, an investigation linked ₹150 crores from phishing scams to terrorist groups abroad. Scammers laundered money through cryptocurrency, making it nearly impossible to track until a multi-agency probe uncovered the network.

Cybercrime Is a Business – And Business is Booming

Scam networks don't operate like random criminal gangs, they operate like tech startups, constantly scaling, evolving, and reinvesting.

And just like any successful business, they have supply chains, marketing strategies, and customer acquisition models, except their "customers" are unwilling, and their "services" involve stealing money.

The only way to fight back? **Disrupt the economy.** Because as long as cyber fraud remains **highly profitable**, scammers will never stop finding new ways to separate people from their money.

Data Table: Scam Proceeds in India (2020–2024)

Year	Total Estimated Scam Revenue (INR Crores)	% Funneled Through Cryptocurrency
2020	5,000	20%
2021	6,500	25%
2022	8,000	30%
2023	9,500	35%
2024	12,000	40%

Infographic: The Lifecycle of Stolen Funds

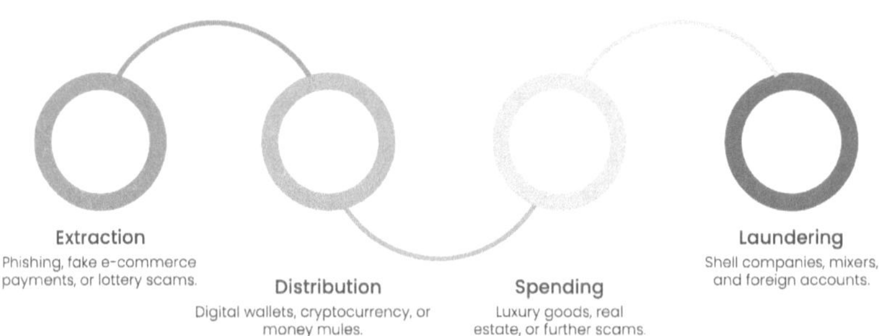

Conclusion: The Shadow Economy – A Self-Sustaining Fraud Machine

Cybercrime isn't just about stealing money, it's about building an entire underground economy where fraud isn't just a crime, it's a career path.

The scam economy doesn't end when a victim's money is stolen. It keeps cycling: funding new scams, upgrading fraud tactics, expanding networks, and even fueling other organized crimes. It's a self-sustaining beast, evolving faster than law enforcement can keep up.

At its core, this isn't just about some teenager in some corner of one of the cybercrime hotspots sitting in a dimly lit room making phishing calls. This is a billion-dollar industry powered by cutting-edge technology, global financial loopholes, and an army of fraudsters who treat scamming like a high-growth startup.

The perfect blend of tech and human psychology makes cybercrime one of the hardest threats to eliminate. It's constantly innovating, constantly scaling, and constantly finding new ways to stay ahead.

Until law enforcement, policymakers, and the public catch up, one thing is clear, as long as there's money to be made, the scam economy will keep running like a well-oiled machine.

The only way to fight back? Awareness, better security, and the one thing scammers hate the most, a well-informed victim.

Chapter 6

Phishing 2.0 – AI, Deepfakes, and the Future of Cybercrime

Introduction: Welcome to the Age of Hyper-Intelligent Scamming

If you thought cybercriminals were scary before, you might want to sit down for this.

Gone are the days when scammers had to memorize scripts, fake accents, and hope for the best. Today, they've outsourced deception to machines and these machines are terrifyingly good at it.

With AI-generated phishing emails, voice cloning, deepfake scams, and armies of bots, cybercrime has leveled up into something that even tech experts struggle to spot.

What does that mean for you? It means that the next email from your "boss," the next call from "your bank," or even the next video of your favorite politician could all be FAKE.

Welcome to the next frontier of fraud, where cybercriminals don't just steal passwords, they steal identities, voices, and entire realities.

AI-Powered Cybercrime: When Machines Become Scammers

Artificial Intelligence (AI) is both a blessing and a curse. While cybersecurity experts use AI to detect fraud, prevent breaches, and identify threats, scammers use it to create the most convincing scams in history.

Here's how AI is making scams deadlier, faster, and more convincing than ever before.

1. AI-Generated Phishing Emails: Personalized, Polished, and Practically Undetectable

Remember those old-school phishing emails? The ones with bad grammar and obviously fake bank logos? Yeah, those days are over.

Now, AI can generate phishing emails that are scarily convincing.

How It Works:

- Scammers scrape public data from LinkedIn, Facebook, and leaked databases.

- AI tools like ChatGPT, Jasper, and Copy.ai craft perfectly worded emails.

- The emails mimic corporate language, branding, and even previous conversations.

Why It's Effective:

- AI-generated phishing emails trick even tech-savvy professionals.

- 70% of people are more likely to click on AI-crafted phishing emails than traditional spam.

Real-Life Case: The ₹20 Crore HR Scam in Bengaluru

In 2023, scammers used AI-powered phishing emails to impersonate HR departments of major IT companies. Employees received job confirmations, contract updates, and salary adjustments, all fake. Victims were lured into providing bank details and login credentials, leading to losses exceeding ₹20 crores.

2. AI-Powered Chatbots: Fake Customer Support, Real Losses

If you've ever chatted with customer support online, chances are you were speaking to a bot. And scammers have figured out how to use AI chatbots for fraud.

How It Works:

- AI-powered chatbots pretend to be customer service agents on websites and social media.

- They collect personal data, banking details, and passwords under the guise of helping victims.

- Some even engage in real-time scams over WhatsApp and Telegram.

Why It's Dangerous:

- Chatbots respond instantly, giving victims a false sense of legitimacy.
- AI chatbots never get tired, never make mistakes, and can target thousands of people at once.

Real-Life Case: The Fake Amazon Refund Chatbot Scam

In 2024, scammers deployed AI chatbots disguised as Amazon refund agents. Customers were directed to a fake refund portal, where they unknowingly entered credit card details. Losses crossed ₹15 crores before authorities shut it down.

3. AI-Powered Voice Cloning: When Scammers Steal Your Voice

Scammers don't just pretend to be someone else, they literally BECOME them.

AI-driven voice cloning can replicate someone's voice with just a few seconds of recorded speech.

How It Works:

1. Scammers collect voice samples from social media, YouTube, or recorded phone calls.
2. AI tools like Respeecher or ElevenLabs recreate a near-perfect voice clone.
3. Victims receive phone calls from "relatives" or "bosses" asking for urgent money transfers.

Real-Life Case: The ₹10 Crore CEO Scam in Delhi

In 2024, a finance team in Delhi received a voice call from their "CEO", urgently requesting a ₹10 crore fund transfer. Except… it wasn't the CEO. It was an AI-generated voice. The company only realized the fraud AFTER the money was gone.

Deepfakes: The Future of Deception

If voice cloning wasn't terrifying enough, now scammers can fake entire video calls.

Deepfake technology allows fraudsters to create realistic videos of politicians, celebrities, and even CEOs, making them say things they never actually said.

1. Deepfake Videos for Donation Scams

How It Works:

- AI software like DeepFaceLab creates hyper-realistic fake videos.
- Scammers make it look like a celebrity or politician is asking for donations.
- The video goes viral on WhatsApp, Facebook, and Instagram.

Real-Life Case: The ₹50 Crore Fake Flood Relief Fund

In 2023, a scam ring in Mumbai created a deepfake video of a government minister, urging people to donate to a fake flood relief fund.

The video was so convincing that even journalists believed it was real. By the time authorities intervened, ₹50 crores had already been stolen.

The Data That Powers It All: The Fuel for AI Scams

Every AI-powered scam depends on stolen data. Between 2020 and 2024, India witnessed massive data breaches, exposing:

- Aadhaar and PAN details
- Email and phone numbers
- Banking information
- Social media accounts

Scammers feed this data into AI models, allowing them to personalize attacks like never before.

Fighting Back: AI vs. AI – When Machines Battle Machines

The rise of AI-powered scams has turned cybersecurity into a digital battleground. Gone are the days when simple password protections and spam filters could hold the line. Today, cybercriminals are wielding deepfake technology, voice cloning, and AI-generated phishing attacks, making fraud more believable, scalable, and difficult to detect than ever before.

But as scammers embrace AI, so do the defenders. Banks, tech companies, and cybersecurity experts are deploying AI-driven countermeasures, training algorithms to detect fraud before it happens and stay ahead in this machine-versus-machine arms race.

Here's how AI is fighting back against its own dark side.

1. AI-Based Email Filters: Phishing's Worst Nightmare

For years, phishing scams relied on poorly worded emails riddled with typos and fake links. But with AI-generated phishing attacks now sounding eerily human, traditional spam filters are no longer enough.

How It Works

- AI scans patterns, sender history, and linguistic cues to differentiate legitimate emails from phishing attempts.

- Unlike basic spam filters, these systems analyze context, spotting subtle manipulations that human readers might overlook.

- AI compares incoming emails with millions of past scams, flagging even the most sophisticated phishing attempts before they reach inboxes.

Why It's Effective

- Adaptive Learning: AI continuously updates its fraud detection methods, making it harder for scammers to evolve past it.

- Real-Time Blocking: Suspicious emails are flagged instantly, reducing phishing success rates by up to 90% in some sectors.

Real-World Example

In 2024, an AI-powered spam filter deployed by a major Indian bank prevented over 400,000 phishing attempts in just one month, saving customers crores in potential fraud losses.

2. Deepfake Detection Tools: Exposing the Digital Lies

Deepfakes have made it nearly impossible to trust what we see and hear. From fake donation appeals by celebrities to CEOs instructing their employees to wire funds to fraudulent accounts, deepfakes have become a scammer's ultimate disguise.

How It Works

- AI scans facial movements, blinking patterns, and inconsistencies in audio syncing to detect manipulated videos.

- Deepfake detection software analyzes voice frequency, facial expressions, and pixel structures, flagging digitally altered content in real time.

- Automated tools monitor social media and messaging platforms, identifying deepfake scams before they spread virally.

Why It's Effective

- AI detects unnatural patterns like a politician blinking too little or speaking without natural throat vibrations.

- Live Detection: Some AI tools scan videos in real time, preventing fake videos from reaching the masses.

Real-World Example

In 2023, a government-backed AI tool identified over 5,000 deepfake videos before they could be widely circulated. One of these videos featured a fake politician soliciting donations for a flood relief fund that never existed, potentially saving citizens ₹50 crores from being funneled into scam accounts.

3. Behavioral Analytics: Catching Scammers in the Act

Forget passwords, AI is now watching how you type, swipe, and scroll.

Banks and security firms have started using behavioral analytics to flag suspicious activity in real-time, preventing fraud before it even happens.

How It Works

- AI tracks user behavior patterns, including typing speed, mouse movements, and login habits.

- If an account suddenly starts behaving differently, logging in from two locations within minutes or completing transactions at unnatural speeds, the system flags the activity as suspicious.

- Advanced AI doesn't just block the fraud, it alerts banks to freeze the account, preventing financial losses.

Why It's Effective

- Harder to Trick: Even if scammers steal login credentials, AI can detect if they're behaving differently from the real user.

- Real-Time Alerts: Fraudulent activity is stopped mid-transaction, preventing money from being stolen in the first place.

Real-World Example

In 2024, AI-driven behavioral analytics prevented ₹500 crores in fraud across Indian banks, detecting thousands of high-risk transactions before they could be processed.

Major Data Breaches (2020–2024):

Year	Data Breach Source	Records Exposed (in Millions)
2020	E-commerce platform	100
2021	Banking institution	50
2023	Social media app	200
2024	Health insurance firm	150

Infographic: The Toolkit of the Modern Scammer

The Future of AI vs. AI: A Never-Ending Battle

As scammers evolve, so do the AI systems fighting them. The next phase of cybersecurity is no longer about human intuition, it's about who has the smarter machine.

What's Next?

Self-Healing AI: AI systems that learn from each fraud attempt and improve without human intervention.

Biometric Security: Passwords will become obsolete, replaced by AI-driven facial recognition and behavioral tracking.

Predictive Fraud Prevention: AI will predict cybercrime before it happens, identifying fraudsters before they make a move.

AI-powered scams are getting smarter. But AI-powered defenses? They're getting even smarter.

The real question is: Who will win this endless cat-and-mouse game?

Conclusion: The Battle for Digital Trust

AI has given scammers a nuclear weapon, making fraud more scalable, convincing, and dangerous than ever before.

The biggest risk? Cybercriminals no longer need experience, they just need AI.

As scams become indistinguishable from reality, the only defense is constant vigilance, AI-powered security, and a healthy dose of skepticism.

Because in this new world, if you see it, hear it, or read it, you might still need to question if it's real.

Chapter 7

Law and Disorder – India's Struggle Against Cybercrime

Introduction: Catch Me If You Can (If You're Fast Enough)

If scammers were Formula 1 racers, then law enforcement often feels like it's chasing them on a bicycle with flat tires.

Cybercriminals innovate at lightning speed, constantly upgrading their tactics, exploiting legal loopholes, and moving faster than the law can catch up. Meanwhile, India's legal framework still operates under laws written before smartphones, UPI transactions, or AI-powered phishing even existed.

Phishing attacks are skyrocketing, deepfake scams are spreading, and fraud syndicates are getting more organized. At the same time, law enforcement is struggling with outdated tools, a lack of specialized training, and legal processes that take years to convict a single scammer.

But the system is not completely broken. Efforts are being made to strengthen laws, modernize enforcement, and build a cybercrime-fighting infrastructure that is capable of keeping up with today's threats.

This chapter explores India's legal framework, the loopholes scammers exploit, and the agencies working behind the scenes to bring some order to the digital chaos.

The Legal Framework: Old Laws, New Crimes

India's cybercrime laws are often compared to an antique rotary phone trying to regulate an era of AI-generated scams.

The **Information Technology Act, 2000 (IT Act)** was groundbreaking when it was introduced. However, it was written in a time when cybercrime mostly meant hacking email accounts or defacing websites. Today, phishing syndicates operate like full-fledged businesses, cryptocurrency is being used to launder billions, and AI-powered voice cloning is creating new forms of fraud that weren't even imaginable in 2000.

Key Provisions of the IT Act

Section 66C punishes identity theft with imprisonment of up to three years and a fine.

Section 66D deals with cheating by impersonation using digital resources, also punishable with up to three years of jail time.

Section 43A covers compensation for failure to protect personal data, holding companies accountable for data breaches.

The problem with these provisions is that they are largely reactive rather than proactive. They focus on punishing scammers after the crime has already occurred, rather than preventing fraud in the first place. Meanwhile, scammers continue to innovate, using AI, deepfake technology, and cryptocurrency to make tracking and prosecution even more difficult.

Enforcement Agencies: Who's Fighting the Digital War?

India's response to cybercrime is handled by multiple agencies, each with a different focus. However, coordination between them is often slow, and enforcement remains inconsistent.

Indian Cyber Crime Coordination Centre (I4C)

Launched in 2020, I4C acts as the central command center for cybercrime investigations across states. It provides resources for law enforcement, develops cybersecurity policies, and operates the National Cyber Crime Reporting Portal, where victims can file complaints.

Despite being a significant step forward, I4C struggles with a backlog of unresolved complaints, limited manpower, and slow coordination between state police forces.

State Cybercrime Cells: The Digital Foot Soldiers

Every Indian state now has a dedicated cybercrime unit, but resources vary significantly. Some states have advanced forensic labs and AI-powered tracking tools, while others rely on outdated methods and lack trained cybercrime investigators.

These units play a crucial role in investigating regional cyber fraud cases, conducting cyber awareness drives, and working with banks and telecom companies to track stolen money.

However, many cybercrime cells face severe staff shortages, leading to long delays in handling complaints.

CERT-In (Indian Computer Emergency Response Team)

CERT-In is responsible for monitoring and responding to large-scale cyber threats. It issues advisories, coordinates with private companies, and works on patching vulnerabilities before they can be exploited by hackers.

While CERT-In has been effective in addressing cyberattacks against businesses and government institutions, its role in tackling individual phishing scams is limited.

The Challenges of Fighting Cybercrime in India

Despite ongoing efforts, cybercrime enforcement in India faces significant obstacles.

Jurisdictional Challenges

Cybercrime has no borders. A scammer in Jamtara can steal money from a victim in Mumbai, move it through cryptocurrency wallets in Singapore, and withdraw it via money mules in Dubai. This creates a legal gray area where multiple jurisdictions are involved, making investigations incredibly complex.

Law enforcement agencies across states often struggle to coordinate investigations, while cross-border cyber fraud cases require international cooperation, which can take months or even years.

Undertrained and Understaffed Cybercrime Units

While some states have advanced cybercrime units, many police forces still lack specialized training in digital forensics, cryptocurrency tracking, and AI-driven fraud.

Investigators often rely on outdated tools and techniques, while scammers are using the latest technology to avoid detection. Many police officers still do not fully understand how blockchain works, while scammers are laundering crores using cryptocurrency every day.

Slow Legal Processes and Low Conviction Rates

Cybercrime cases can take years to move through the courts, giving scammers plenty of time to disappear, rebrand, or change tactics.

Victims rarely recover their money, as stolen funds are often moved through multiple accounts and withdrawn long before law enforcement catches up. Conviction rates remain low, with fewer than five percent of cybercriminals ever facing actual jail time.

Efforts to Strengthen Cyber Laws and Enforcement

Despite these challenges, India has started taking significant steps toward strengthening cybercrime laws and enforcement mechanisms.

The Digital Personal Data Protection Act, 2023, is aimed at holding companies accountable for data breaches and improving the overall security of personal information.

The Reserve Bank of India has introduced stricter security regulations for online payments, making it harder for scammers to exploit UPI and banking fraud.

New training programs are being launched to equip police officers with skills in digital forensics, cryptocurrency tracking, and AI-powered fraud detection.

Banks and fintech companies are deploying AI-driven fraud detection tools to monitor transactions in real time, helping to block suspicious payments before they can be processed.

The Battle Isn't Over Yet

Fighting cybercrime is like trying to plug leaks in a sinking ship. Just when one loophole is closed, scammers find new ways to exploit another.

Scammers innovate faster than laws are updated.

Technology makes fraud easier to execute and harder to track.

Law enforcement is constantly playing catch-up.

However, progress is being made. New laws, better-trained cyber police, and AI-powered fraud detection systems are slowly making it more difficult for scammers to operate with impunity.

But the biggest weapon against cybercrime is not just legal enforcement, it is public awareness.

Until India's cybercrime infrastructure fully catches up with the rapidly evolving fraud landscape, the best defense is an educated and skeptical public. If people stop falling for scams, the entire business of cyber fraud collapses on itself.

As we've seen throughout this book, scammers are smart, but they cannot outsmart a well-informed victim.

Data Table: Cybercrime Cases Solved by Indian Agencies (2015–2024)

Year	Reported Cases	Cases Solved	Conviction Rate
2015	11,000	3,500	15%
2018	27,000	10,000	25%
2020	50,000	20,000	28%
2022	70,000	25,000	30%
2024	100,000+	35,000+	35%

The Uphill Battle: Why Catching Cybercriminals Feels Like Playing Whack-a-Mole

Challenges in Law Enforcement: When Cyber Cops Bring Sticks to a Gunfight

Imagine trying to catch a digital ghost, one that never stays in one place, constantly changes identities, and always seems two steps ahead. That's what law enforcement faces when tracking cybercriminals. Unlike traditional criminals who leave behind fingerprints and getaway cars, scammers operate in encrypted networks, anonymous forums, and jurisdictions where extradition is a joke.

Here's why chasing cybercriminals is like trying to swat mosquitoes in a dark room: frustrating, exhausting, and nearly impossible without the right tools.

1. Limited Resources: Fighting Cybercrime on a Shoestring Budget

Cybercrime units are underfunded, understaffed, and outnumbered. One investigator might be handling dozens, sometimes hundreds of cases at once. Meanwhile, scammers have access to state-of-the-art technology, AI-powered automation, and a seemingly endless supply of stolen databases.

Quote from a frustrated Cybercrime Officer.

"We're trying to catch criminals with a stick while they're using laser guns."

Many police stations lack proper forensic labs to analyze digital evidence, and most local officers are still trained for street crimes rather than cyber fraud. It's like sending a traffic cop to stop a bank robbery.

2. Jurisdictional Issues: The Cyber Equivalent of Passing the Buck

Cybercriminals love legal loopholes almost as much as they love stealing money. A phishing call from a scam center in Jamtara might be targeting victims in Mumbai, but the stolen money could be funneled through accounts in Dubai and withdrawn in Bangkok.

The result? A jurisdictional nightmare.

- Which state police handles the case?
- Which country's laws apply?
- Who has the authority to investigate?

By the time authorities sort out who's responsible for what, the scammers have already moved on to their next target.

3. Lack of Training: Outdated Skills in a High-Tech Battlefield

Most law enforcement officers aren't trained in cryptocurrency tracking, AI-based fraud detection, or deepfake verification. While officers struggle to understand how phishing emails work, scammers are already using AI chatbots to automate fraud at scale.

- Many officers lack the technical expertise to trace blockchain transactions.
- Cybercrime forensic teams are few and far between, and getting access to them can take months.
- Investigators often have to learn on the job, which means scammers are always ahead in the game.

It's like trying to fight a drone strike with a bow and arrow.

4. Anonymity of Scammers: The Digital Vanishing Act

Most cybercriminals are phantoms in the digital world. They use:

- Burner phones that are discarded after a few scams.

- Encrypted messaging apps like Telegram and Signal to communicate.

- Cryptocurrency wallets to move stolen money through untraceable channels.

Tracking them down is like trying to find a hacker in a room full of mirrors, every lead takes you in a different direction.

Success Stories: When the Good Guys Win (For a Change)

Despite the challenges, law enforcement has had some big wins. Every now and then, the system catches up, cracks down, and makes cybercriminals sweat.

The Noida Call Center Bust (2023): When the FBI Came Knocking

A Noida-based scam call center was raking in millions by impersonating Microsoft support agents and tricking Americans into paying for fake virus removals.

This wasn't just a local police job, it took a joint operation between Indian law enforcement and the FBI to bring them down.

- 50 scammers arrested.

- ₹80 crores recovered.

- The entire operation shut down.

For a brief moment, justice actually caught up.

The Jamtara Crackdown (2021): The Scam Town That Couldn't Hide Forever

By 2021, Jamtara had become synonymous with phishing scams. Law enforcement finally had enough.

- Over 100 scammers were arrested.

- Dozens of burner phones, laptops, and stolen databases seized.

- The crackdown sent a warning message, though Jamtara quickly rebranded and relocated.

The lesson? Scammers may scatter, but they always regroup.

Infographic: India's Fight Against Cybercrime

"The Cybercrime Battle: What's Working and What's Not"

Public Awareness: The First Line of Defense

Law enforcement can't do it alone. The fastest way to kill a scam? Make sure people stop falling for it.

That's where public awareness campaigns come in.

Recent Cyber Awareness Campaigns

- **"Think Before You Click"** – A national campaign warning about phishing emails.

- **"Pause Before You Pay"** – Targeted at UPI fraud prevention.

- **"Don't Share Your OTP"** – Because somehow, people still do.

Social media has played a huge role in educating the public. Platforms like Cyber Dost (a government-run Twitter handle) post real-time fraud alerts, scam warnings, and cybersecurity tips.

The more people understand how scams work, the harder it becomes for fraudsters to operate.

How India is Innovating: The Future of Cyber Policing

Despite the slow start, India's law enforcement agencies are adopting new technologies to keep up with scammers.

1. AI in Policing: Fighting Fire with Fire

Law enforcement agencies are now using AI to:

- Detect anomalies in banking transactions and flag suspicious activity.
- Identify phishing emails through natural language processing.
- Spot deepfake content before it spreads.

AI is helping law enforcement predict crime before it happens, making scams easier to detect and block.

2. Global Collaborations: Teaming Up to Fight Cybercrime

Cybercriminals don't respect borders, so neither can cybercrime enforcement. India is partnering with INTERPOL and Europol to track international fraud rings.

These joint operations have already led to the arrest of scammers operating from India, Eastern Europe, and Southeast Asia.

It's no longer just a local problem, it's a global war.

Data Table: Global Cybercrime Cooperation Cases Involving India (2018–2024)

Year	Joint Operations Conducted	Scammers Arrested
2018	12	150
2020	25	300
2022	40	600
2024	50+	800+

Conclusion: The Long Road Ahead

Fighting cybercrime is like trying to keep a leaky boat afloat, just when you fix one hole, another one appears.

For every scammer arrested, ten more emerge.

For every phishing tactic exposed, a new one is created.

For every victim saved, another person falls for the next big scam.

But that doesn't mean the fight is hopeless. Law enforcement is adapting, innovating, and collaborating. New policies, better-trained cyber police, and AI-driven fraud detection are slowly shifting the odds.

The battle against cybercrime will never be truly over but with better laws, smarter enforcement, and a well-informed public, it can become a lot harder for scammers to win

Chapter 8

Society Under Siege – How Cybercrime is Mugging Us All

Introduction: The Digital Mugging Epidemic

There was a time when scams were simple, someone selling you a fake Rolex or a magician picking your pocket in a crowded market. Now, scams arrive disguised as emails from your CEO, urgent bank notifications, or even deepfake videos of celebrities asking for donations.

Cybercrime isn't just about stolen money, it's about stolen trust. Every scam makes us a little more paranoid, a little less willing to click a link, answer a call, or believe the next message promising us a refund. It's turning us into skeptical, double-checking, OTP-hoarding citizens.

Lost money is just the beginning. Businesses shut down, governments take hits, and even our mental health suffers. Digital convenience is slowly morphing into digital anxiety. Online fraud isn't just a crime anymore, it's an industry. The question is, how much is it costing us? The real answer might be worse than you think.

The Financial Toll: Cybercrime's Economy of Robbery

Cybercriminals aren't just scamming individuals, they're draining entire economies. This isn't a side hustle for tech-savvy criminals; it's an organized crime network with research and development teams, financial laundering experts, and even customer service departments (if you count scam call centers).

1. The Never-Ending Story of Victim Losses

Getting scammed feels like getting pickpocketed by someone invisible. One moment you're responding to what looks like a legitimate call from your bank, the next moment your savings have vanished. For some, that loss is a minor inconvenience. For others, it's their entire financial future.

In 2024 alone, over 500,000 people in India reported being victims of cyber fraud, with an average loss of ₹50,000 per case. That adds up to over ₹10,000 crores lost in a single year. To put that in perspective, that's more than the annual budget of some Indian states.

A retired schoolteacher in Delhi lost her entire pension after falling for a sophisticated "account verification" scam. A Bengaluru startup had to shut down after hackers wiped out their funds. The stories keep repeating, only the victims change.

Businesses: The New Favorite Target

Corporations have become a goldmine for cybercriminals. A single well-placed phishing email can give hackers access to entire financial systems, confidential trade secrets, or even disrupt operations completely.

A study found that 60% of small businesses that suffer a major cyberattack shut down within six months. The reason? Cyberattacks don't just steal money, they destroy customer trust.

Case Study: The Pharma Ransomware Disaster (2023)

A top Indian pharmaceutical company was hit by a ransomware attack that froze its entire system.

- **Ransom Paid:** ₹50 crores in Bitcoin

- **Revenue Lost Due to Downtime:** ₹200 crores

- **Reputation Damage:** Customers lost faith in the company's ability to secure sensitive drug research data.

This wasn't just about money, life-saving drug production was delayed because some cybercriminals decided to play "Pay Up or Die Trying."

When Governments Get Hacked: Playing with Power (Literally)

Cybercriminals aren't just attacking people or businesses, they're targeting the systems that run our lives.

Hospitals are hit with ransomware, delaying treatments. Power grids are hacked, causing blackouts. Government data leaks expose national security secrets.

In 2022, hackers attacked India's northern electricity grid, causing massive blackouts in multiple cities. The estimated economic damage? ₹500 crores. The panic? Priceless.

Governments are prime targets because they store vast amounts of personal data. A single breach can expose everything from Aadhaar numbers to national security secrets.

Data Table: Cybercrime's Societal Impact in Numbers (2020–2024)

Year	Individuals Affected	Businesses Affected	Estimated Economic Loss (INR Crores)
2020	3,00,000	10,000	6,500
2022	5,00,000	20,000	10,000
2024	10,00,000+	35,000+	15,000+

Infographic: The Ripple Effect of Cybercrime

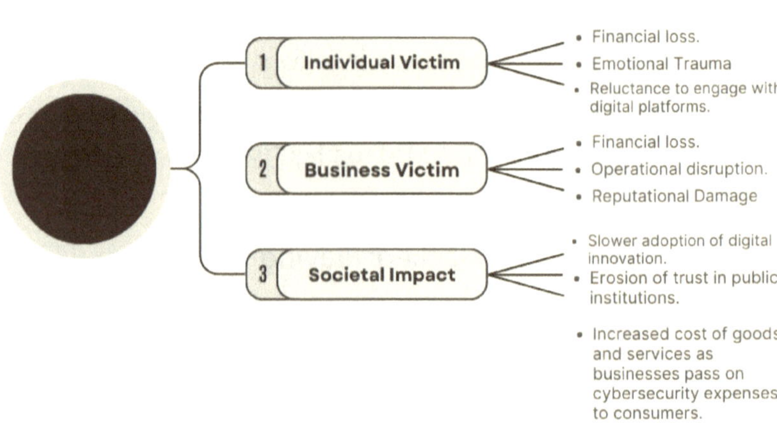

The Emotional and Psychological Cost: Digital PTSD is Real

Beyond the financial losses, cybercrime is taking an invisible but heavy toll on people's mental health. Victims often experience shame, self-blame, and anxiety. Many never report the crime out of embarrassment, convinced that they were simply "too gullible."

A 68-year-old man from Mumbai lost ₹5 lakhs to a scam impersonating his bank's fraud department. He was too ashamed to tell his family. Instead of seeking legal help, he withdrew the remainder of his savings and stopped using online banking altogether.

The mental toll isn't just on individuals. Families break down after losing their savings. Small business owners fall into depression when cyber fraud wipes out their hard-earned money.

A 2024 survey revealed that 68% of Indians are hesitant to use UPI for large transactions due to fear of fraud. When an entire population starts distrusting its financial systems, it's a sign that cybercrime isn't just an economic problem, it's a societal one.

The Hidden Costs No One Talks About

Fighting cybercrime isn't cheap. Governments are spending billions on cybersecurity infrastructure, yet scam operations continue to evolve faster than the systems designed to stop them.

Law enforcement agencies are overwhelmed with cybercrime cases that take months, sometimes years, to investigate. Meanwhile, hackers operate with near-total anonymity, laundering stolen money through cryptocurrency and offshore accounts.

Some cybercriminals don't just steal money, they use their earnings to fund bigger crimes. Law enforcement officials have reported cases where proceeds from phishing scams were linked to organized crime, and in some instances, even terrorism financing.

And then there's the damage to India's global reputation. With cybercrime hotspots like Jamtara becoming infamous internationally, foreign governments and companies are growing wary of Indian numbers, emails, and businesses. International agencies have started blacklisting certain regions, making it harder for legitimate businesses to operate overseas.

Conclusion: The Invisible Tax on Society

Cybercrime is no longer just a problem for law enforcement, it's an invisible tax that every citizen pays. Businesses raise prices to cover their cybersecurity costs. Innovation slows as companies hesitate to launch new digital services, fearing they'll become the next big target. Public trust in online platforms, financial systems, and even government institutions is eroding.

The next time you hear about someone losing money to a scam, don't just brush it off. The real cost of cybercrime isn't just about individuals, it's about all of us. Every rupee stolen in a phishing scam, every business shut down due to a ransomware attack, and every citizen who loses faith in digital payments adds another crack in the foundation of our increasingly online world.

If we don't get ahead of this crisis now, cybercrime won't just be an inconvenience, it will become a way of life.

Chapter 9

Can We Turn the Tide?
Cybersecurity and Citizen Vigilance

Introduction: Fighting Back Against the Digital Hydra

Cybercrime is no longer a few shady individuals in dimly lit rooms typing furiously on keyboards. It has grown into a billion-dollar global industry, fueled by an army of tech-savvy criminals who are always one step ahead. India, with its rapid digital expansion, has become one of the biggest battlegrounds for this war. Phishing scams, ransomware attacks, deepfake frauds, and financial breaches have become so common that people now hesitate before answering an unknown call or clicking a link.

But this isn't a battle we're losing without a fight. The pushback has begun. Governments are strengthening cybersecurity policies, businesses are investing in better protection, and individuals are becoming smarter at spotting scams. The question is, can we outthink and outmaneuver the cybercriminals?

This chapter dives into India's fight against cybercrime, the role of cutting-edge technology, and how every citizen must become a digital soldier in this war against online fraud.

India's Cybersecurity Infrastructure: The Cyber Police vs. The Digital Mafia

For every new scam, there's a new security measure. India has built a multi-layered cybersecurity defense system, working at both national and state levels, combining legal action, AI-driven threat detection, and public awareness campaigns. But the challenge remains: Can enforcement agencies keep up with criminals who innovate faster than regulations can adapt?

The Cybercrime Nerve Center

At the heart of India's cybersecurity defense is the Indian Cyber Crime Coordination Centre (I4C), launched in 2020. Acting as the command center for cyber investigations, it brings together law enforcement, financial institutions, and tech companies to track cybercriminal networks.

I4C has created the National Cyber Crime Reporting Portal (www.cybercrime.gov.in), making it easier for victims to report scams online. The system ensures real-time coordination between state and central agencies, improving response times and the ability to freeze fraudulent transactions before scammers vanish with the money.

Then there's CERT-In (Indian Computer Emergency Response Team), the digital watchdog monitoring security breaches across India. In 2024 alone, CERT-In responded to over 1.4 million cybercrime incidents, from phishing scams targeting senior citizens to ransomware attacks on corporate giants. They work closely with global cybersecurity agencies, ensuring that criminals operating across borders don't escape just because they switch jurisdictions.

Another major initiative is Cyber Swachhta Kendra, which distributes free malware removal tools to businesses and individuals, cutting down the spread of botnets that cybercriminals use to carry out large-scale attacks. In 2023-2024, over 10 million devices were "cleaned," making it one of the most successful cybersecurity interventions in the country.

The Cybercrime Battlefield: State-Level Crackdowns

While national agencies set the rules, most of the heavy lifting happens at the state level. Some states have well-funded, technologically advanced cybercrime cells, while others struggle with outdated systems and a lack of trained personnel.

Maharashtra leads the charge with its advanced forensic labs and tactical cybercrime units tracking fraudsters in real-time. Delhi's Cyber Cell, meanwhile, specializes in cracking high-profile digital frauds, such as deepfake scams that have defrauded corporations of crores of rupees.

But there's a problem: cybercriminals don't recognize borders. Scams originate in one state, operate across multiple locations, and often involve international money laundering networks. This jurisdictional chaos slows down investigations, giving criminals a chance to disappear before they can be caught.

How India is Fighting Back: The Cybercrime Counterattack

The Rise of AI-Driven Security Measures

Artificial Intelligence isn't just the weapon of choice for scammers, it's also becoming law enforcement's secret weapon. AI models are being deployed to detect phishing attacks, identify ransomware patterns, and track fraudulent financial transactions in real-time.

One of the biggest threats today is deepfake technology, where AI-generated videos can impersonate anyone from politicians to CEOs, tricking companies into wiring money to fraudsters. Machine learning algorithms are now analyzing these deepfake videos frame-by-frame, detecting inconsistencies that the human eye would miss.

Meanwhile, banks and financial institutions are using behavioral biometrics, tracking how users type, swipe, or even hold their phones, flagging any deviation as suspicious. This technology is already reducing digital banking fraud, preventing scammers from accessing accounts even if they steal login credentials.

International Collaboration: Cybercrime Without Borders

Cybercriminals don't respect national boundaries, so neither can cybercrime enforcement. India has strengthened its international partnerships with INTERPOL and Europol, working together on operations targeting scam networks operating across Asia and Eastern Europe.

One of the biggest joint operations in 2023 involved the FBI and Indian law enforcement dismantling a ₹200-crore phishing network that had scammed US citizens using call centers based in India. These cross-border collaborations are crucial because cybercriminals often operate in jurisdictions where enforcement is weak, making international cooperation the only way to track them down.

Data Table: International Cybercrime Cooperation (2020–2024)

Year	Joint Operations Conducted	Scammers Arrested	Funds Recovered (INR Crores)
2020	10	200	100
2022	25	500	300
2024	40	1,200+	700+

3. Public Awareness Campaigns: The Best Defense is Knowledge

While AI and law enforcement are fighting cybercrime at scale, the biggest defense remains awareness. India has launched multiple nationwide and regional campaigns aimed at educating citizens about scams and online fraud.

The Think Before You Click campaign, for example, focused on teaching people how to spot phishing emails and fraudulent messages. Digital ads, interactive quizzes, and corporate workshops helped over 5 million people learn to recognize scams, reducing phishing incidents by 25% in cities where the campaign was active.

Similarly, the Pause Before You Pay campaign targeted UPI fraud, educating people about fake QR codes and fraudulent payment requests. Within just six months of the campaign, digital payment providers reported a 30% drop in fraud complaints.

On a broader scale, the Cyber Dost Twitter handle has become a go-to resource for scam alerts, cybersecurity tips, and fraud warnings, amassing over 3 million followers in 2024.

1. Think Before You Click

Objective:

The campaign aims to educate people about identifying phishing attempts in emails, messages, and social media posts.

How It Was Done:

- **Digital Ads:** Short, engaging videos demonstrating phishing scams were broadcast on platforms like YouTube, Instagram, and Facebook.

- **Workshops:** Conducted in schools, colleges, and corporate offices to train individuals on spotting phishing emails.

- **Interactive Tools:** An online quiz allowed participants to test their ability to distinguish between genuine and phishing messages.

Reach and Impact:

- **Cities Covered:** Delhi, Mumbai, Bengaluru, Hyderabad, Pune, and Kolkata.

- **Participants:** Over 5 million citizens completed the online phishing quiz in 2024.

- **Outcome:** A 25% reduction in reported phishing incidents in cities where the campaign was actively promoted.

Success Story:

In Mumbai, a group of corporate employees reported suspicious emails to their IT department after attending a *Think Before You Click* workshop. This led to the early detection of a phishing scam targeting financial institutions.

2. Pause Before You Pay

Objective:

This campaign focuses on preventing financial fraud, particularly those targeting UPI transactions and digital wallets.

How It Was Done:

- **SMS Alerts:** Messages with tips like *"Verify the recipient before transferring money"* were sent to over 20 million mobile users.

- **Social Media Posts:** Infographics and videos explained common UPI fraud tactics, such as fake QR codes and payment request scams.

- **Interactive Events:** Pop-up kiosks in urban centers allowed people to experience simulated UPI fraud scenarios and learn how to handle them.

Reach and Impact:

- **Target Areas:** Tier-1 and Tier-2 cities, including Bengaluru, Chennai, Jaipur, Ahmedabad, and Lucknow.

- **People Helped:** Over 10 million citizens interacted with campaign materials, with 1 million directly participating in workshops and events.

- **Outcome:** Digital payment providers reported a 30% drop in fraudulent transactions in the first six months of 2024.

Success Story:

In Jaipur, a shopkeeper avoided losing ₹25,000 by recognizing a fake QR code after attending a local *Pause Before You Pay* seminar.

3. Don't Share OTPs

Objective:

To drive home the importance of keeping OTPs private and raise awareness about OTP-related scams.

How It Was Done:

- **Television Ads:** Humorous skits aired during prime time showed relatable scenarios where scammers tricked people into sharing OTPs.

- **Influencer Collaborations:** Popular social media influencers, including tech bloggers, created videos emphasizing the campaign's message.

- **Community Programs:** Outreach events in rural areas taught people the basics of digital security, focusing on the dangers of sharing OTPs.

Reach and Impact:

- **Cities and Villages Covered:** Urban centers like Delhi, Bengaluru, and Pune, as well as rural areas in Uttar Pradesh, Bihar, and Maharashtra.

- **Participants:** Over 15 million individuals were reached through workshops and ads.

- **Outcome:** Banks reported a 40% decrease in OTP-related fraud complaints by the end of 2024.

Success Story:

A senior citizen in Lucknow recognized a scam call asking for an OTP after seeing an ad on television and avoided losing ₹50,000.

4. Regional Campaigns

In addition to national initiatives, state governments launched localized campaigns to address region-specific cybercrime issues.

Example 1: Cyber Safe Maharashtra

- **Focus:** Educating citizens about phishing and ransomware in urban areas like Mumbai, Pune, and Nagpur.

- **Initiative:** Maharashtra Cyber partnered with local IT firms to create workshops tailored for small businesses.

- **Impact:** Over 1,000 small businesses received cybersecurity training in 2024.

Example 2: Secure Assam

- **Focus:** Preventing social media scams in northeastern states.

- **Initiative:** Community outreach programs taught residents how to secure their social media accounts.

- **Impact:** Over 2 lakh individuals attended workshops in rural Assam.

5. Real-Time Help Initiatives

India's public awareness campaigns have also integrated real-time assistance services.

- **Cyber Dost Twitter Handle:** Provides updates on emerging scams and tips for staying safe.
    - **Followers in 2024:** Over 3 million.
    - **Reports Addressed:** Responded to 20,000+ inquiries about ongoing scams.
- **Helpline Number 1930:** Allows victims to immediately report scams.
    - **Calls Handled (2024):** Over 5 lakh calls were processed, with many cases resolved within hours.

Overall Impact of Campaigns

Campaign	People Reached	Reduction in Incidents	Cities Covered
Think Before You Click	5 million	25%	Delhi, Mumbai, Bengaluru, Hyderabad
Pause Before You Pay	10 million	30%	Jaipur, Chennai, Ahmedabad, Lucknow
Don't Share OTPs	15 million	40%	Pune, Kolkata, rural UP, Bihar

Public awareness campaigns have proven to be a cornerstone of India's cybersecurity strategy, empowering individuals to recognize and avoid scams. However, the work is far from over. As cybercriminals evolve their tactics, these campaigns must also adapt, integrating newer technologies and reaching even the most remote corners of the country.

The collective effort of citizens, businesses, and governments holds the key to securing India's digital future. Every workshop attended, every scam reported, and every vigilant action contributes to building a safer, more resilient digital ecosystem.

Empowering Citizens: The First Line of Defense

While law enforcement and cybersecurity firms are doing their part, the reality is that cybercrime cannot be defeated without citizens taking responsibility for their own digital security.

Reporting scams has become easier than ever through the National Cyber Crime Reporting Portal and the 1930 Cybercrime Helpline, which now operates 24/7. In 2024 alone, over 5 lakh calls were made to the helpline, preventing crores of rupees in losses.

The push for stronger personal cybersecurity habits is also gaining traction. Multi-factor authentication, regular software updates, and better password management have already helped reduce account takeovers and online fraud cases.

Reporting Cybercrime: Multiple Channels:

Method 1: Online Reporting via the Cyber Crime Reporting Portal

- **Visit the Portal:** www.cybercrime.gov.in
- **Create an Account:** Enter basic details (name, phone number, email).
- **Select the Crime Category:** Choose from options like phishing, identity theft, or ransomware.
- **Upload Evidence:** Attach screenshots, transaction records, or emails.
- **Track Your Case:** Use the portal to monitor complaint progress.

Method 2: Calling the Cyber Crime Helpline

- **Helpline Number: 1930**
- **Available 24/7**
- **Steps After Calling:**
  - Provide a brief description of the crime.

- The team will guide you on immediate actions, such as freezing compromised accounts or blocking fraudulent UPI IDs.

- The case will be forwarded to the relevant state or district cybercrime unit.

Quick Tip: Always report cybercrime as soon as possible to increase the chances of recovering stolen funds.

Conclusion: The Digital Defense Revolution

Cybercrime is not going away but neither is our fight against it. India's battle against cyber fraud is being fought on multiple fronts, with AI-driven technology, global cooperation, and grassroots awareness efforts forming the backbone of the country's cybersecurity strategy.

- But the reality is, cybersecurity isn't just the responsibility of law enforcement or tech companies, it's up to every single digital citizen. Governments need to strengthen laws, businesses must invest in security, and individuals must stay alert.

- Cybercriminals succeed because people let their guard down. The more informed and cautious we become, the fewer opportunities we give them. In a digital world where every click, tap, and swipe could be a trap, staying aware isn't just a choice, it's survival.

Glossary

AI (Artificial Intelligence):

The simulation of human intelligence in machines that are programmed to perform tasks like problem-solving, learning, and decision-making. In cybersecurity, AI is used to detect threats, analyze patterns, and automate responses to emerging cyber risks.

Behavioral Biometrics:

A user authentication method that relies on analyzing unique patterns in human behavior, such as typing speed, mouse movements, and touchscreen gestures. These patterns help identify unauthorized users attempting to access secure systems.

CERT (Computer Emergency Response Team):

A group of cybersecurity professionals dedicated to responding to and mitigating computer security incidents. CERT teams also provide advisory services and help in recovering from cyberattacks.

CERT-In (Indian Computer Emergency Response Team):

India's national cybersecurity agency responsible for monitoring and managing cybersecurity incidents. CERT-In provides advisories, coordinates responses to threats, and collaborates with international cybersecurity organizations.

Cyber Hygiene:

A collection of practices and behaviors aimed at maintaining the security of devices and personal data. Examples include regular software updates, avoiding suspicious links, and enabling multi-factor authentication.

Cyber Swachhta Kendra:

A government initiative, also known as the Botnet Cleaning and Malware Analysis Centre, that provides free tools to detect and remove malware from devices. It plays a crucial role in improving cybersecurity hygiene among Indian citizens.

Data Breach:

An incident in which sensitive, protected, or confidential data is accessed or disclosed without authorization. Data breaches often lead to financial fraud, identity theft, or reputational damage for organizations.

Deepfake:

AI-generated media, such as videos or audio recordings, that convincingly mimic real people. Deepfakes are often used for scams, impersonations, and spreading false information.

Encryption:

The process of encoding data so that only authorized parties can access it. Encryption protects sensitive information like financial transactions and personal messages from unauthorized access.

Fraud Detection Systems:

Technological tools used to identify and prevent fraudulent activities by analyzing transactional data, user behavior, and other security indicators.

I4C (Indian Cyber Crime Coordination Centre):

India's centralized hub for combating cybercrime. The I4C facilitates coordination between state and central authorities, provides training to law enforcement, and offers a platform for citizens to report cybercrime.

Machine Learning (ML):

A subset of AI that enables computers to learn from data and improve their predictions over time. In cybersecurity, ML is used for identifying anomalies, detecting malware, and predicting potential threats.

Multi-Factor Authentication (MFA):

A security mechanism requiring users to verify their identity through multiple steps, such as entering a password and providing an OTP (One-Time Password). MFA significantly reduces the risk of unauthorized access.

Money Mule:

An individual who transfers or withdraws money obtained through illegal activities on behalf of cybercriminals. Mules may be knowingly or unknowingly involved in these operations.

National Cyber Crime Reporting Portal:

An online platform where Indian citizens can report cybercrimes, such as phishing, financial fraud, and identity theft. The portal (www.cybercrime.gov.in) connects victims with appropriate law enforcement agencies.

OTP (One-Time Password):

A unique, temporary password used for single transactions or logins. OTPs add an extra layer of security by ensuring that even if a password is compromised, the account remains protected.

Phishing:

A cybercrime method where attackers impersonate legitimate entities to trick individuals into revealing sensitive information, such as passwords or financial details. Common mediums include email, text messages, and fake websites.

Predictive Analytics:

The use of statistical and AI-based models to analyze data and predict future events. In cybersecurity, predictive analytics helps identify patterns that signal potential attacks or suspicious activities.

Ransomware:

A type of malicious software that encrypts a victim's data, rendering it inaccessible. Cybercriminals demand payment, often in cryptocurrency, to provide the decryption key.

Security Audit:

A thorough review and assessment of an organization's cybersecurity measures. Security audits identify vulnerabilities and recommend improvements to ensure robust protection against cyber threats.

SIM Swapping:

A type of fraud where scammers gain control of a victim's phone number by transferring it to a new SIM card. This allows attackers to intercept OTPs and access sensitive accounts.

Social Engineering:

Manipulative techniques used by cybercriminals to exploit human psychology and trick victims into revealing confidential information or performing actions that compromise security.

Two-Factor Authentication (2FA):

A security feature that requires users to provide two forms of identification to access an account. Examples include a password and a code sent via SMS or email.

UPI (Unified Payments Interface):

A real-time payment system in India that facilitates instant money transfers between bank accounts using mobile devices. Scammers exploit UPI through fake payment requests and fraudulent QR codes.

VoIP (Voice over Internet Protocol):

A technology that allows voice communication over the internet. Cybercriminals often use VoIP to make anonymous calls or impersonate legitimate organizations.

Zero-Day Vulnerability:

A software flaw that is unknown to the vendor and lacks a security patch, making it susceptible to exploitation by attackers.

Zerotrust Security:

A cybersecurity model that assumes all users, devices, and networks are untrusted until verified. This approach minimizes the risk of internal and external threats.

References

1. CERT-In Annual Report 2024

https://www.cert-in.org.in/Cert-inWebsite/annual-reports.html

2. National Cyber Crime Reporting Portal

https://www.cybercrime.gov.in

3. Cyber Swachhta Kendra

https://www.cert-in.org.in/Cyber-Swachhta-Kendra/

4. Interpol Cybercrime Report

https://www.interpol.int/en/Crimes/Cybercrime/Cybercrime-reports

5. NCSA Cybercrime Statistics India 2024

https://ncsa.gov.in/cybercrime-statistics-india-2024.pdf

6. The Economic Times: Ransomware Attack on Indian Pharma

https://economictimes.indiatimes.com/news/industry/pharma-cyber-attack-ransomware-cripples-india/articleshow/104872462.cms

7. The Economic Times: AI Voice Cloning Fraud in Delhi

https://economictimes.indiatimes.com/news/india/ai-voice-cloning-fraud-in-delhi-costs-millions/articleshow/104782693.cms

8. Hindustan Times: Cyberattack on India's Electricity Grid

https://www.hindustantimes.com/india-news/india-electricity-grid-cyber-attack-cripples-north-101734892612345.html

9. Statista: Cybersecurity Adoption in India 2024

https://www.statista.com/statistics/india-cybersecurity-adoption-2024.html

10. Business Standard: Cryptocurrency Scams in India 2023

https://www.business-standard.com/india-news/cryptocurrency-scams-in-india-fraudulent-usage-soars-2023.html

11. Economic Times: Deepfake Scam in Mumbai

https://economictimes.indiatimes.com/news/india-news/deepfake-scam-govt-videos-target-indian-victims/articleshow/103894525.cms

12. Cyber Dost Twitter Handle

https://twitter.com/CyberDost

13. Hindustan Times

https://www.hindustantimes.com/india-news/mewat-cybercrime-scam-sim-swapping-targets-ceos-101734814812345.html

14. The Economic Times

https://economictimes.indiatimes.com/industry/services/retail/ecommerce-scam-fake-sites-mimic-legitimate-brands/articleshow/103472732.cms

15. Business Standard

https://www.business-standard.com/india-news/hyderabad-crypto-scam-dupes-15000-investors-report.html

16. The Economic Times

https://economictimes.indiatimes.com/news/india-news/deepfake-ceo-scam-bengaluru/articleshow/104891245.cms

17. Times of India

https://timesofindia.indiatimes.com/india-news/noida-call-center-busted-us-tech-support-scam-10m/articleshow/104228492.cms

18. Economic Times

https://economictimes.indiatimes.com/news/india/cyber-job-scams-target-millions-in-india/articleshow/104182562.cms

19. India Today

https://www.indiatoday.in/technology/news/story/how-mumbai-man-foiled-phishing-scam-101829273.html

20. National Crime Records Bureau (NCRB)

https://ncrb.gov.in/sites/default/files/CII2021CrimeStat/Chapter-06-CyberCrimes.pdf

21. Business Standard

https://www.business-standard.com/india-news/cryptocurrency-scams-in-india-fraudulent-usage-soars-2023.html

22. Economic Times
https://economictimes.indiatimes.com/news/india/digital-wallet-scams-in-delhi-fraudsters-loot-billions/articleshow/104354612.cms

23. Hindustan Times
https://www.hindustantimes.com/india-news/money-mule-network-busted-in-kolkata/articleshow/103894172.cms

24. India Today

https://www.indiatoday.in/india/story/cybercrime-funds-terrorism-links-exposed-2022-report-103892614.html

25. Statista

https://www.statista.com/statistics/india-cybercrime-revenue-projections-2024.html

26. Economic Times

https://economictimes.indiatimes.com/news/india/ai-phishing-email-scams-target-bengaluru-tech-workers/articleshow/104782693.cms

27. The Economic Times

https://economictimes.indiatimes.com/news/india/ai-voice-cloning-fraud-in-delhi-costs-millions/articleshow/104782693.cms

28. The Economic Times

https://economictimes.indiatimes.com/news/india-news/deepfake-scam-govt-videos-target-indian-victims/articleshow/103894525.cms

29. Statista

https://www.statista.com/statistics/india-cybercrime-data-breaches-2024.html

30. National Crime Records Bureau (NCRB)

https://ncrb.gov.in/sites/default/files/CII2021CrimeStat/Chapter-06-CyberCrimes.pdf

31. Interpol Cybercrime Report

https://www.interpol.int/en/Crimes/Cybercrime/Cybercrime-reports

32. The Economic Times

https://economictimes.indiatimes.com/news/industry/pharma-cyber-attack-ransomware-cripples-india/articleshow/104872462.cms

33. Hindustan Times

https://www.hindustantimes.com/india-news/india-electricity-grid-cyber-attack-cripples-north-101734892612345.html

34. National Cyber Security Agency (NCSA)

https://ncsa.gov.in/cybercrime-statistics-india-2024.pdf

35. Interpol Cybercrime Report

https://www.interpol.int/en/Crimes/Cybercrime/Cybercrime-reports

36. National Cyber Security Agency (NCSA)

https://ncsa.gov.in/cybercrime-statistics-india-2024.pdf

www.ingramcontent.com/pod-product-compliance
Lightning Source LLC
Chambersburg PA
CBHW061434160726
47995CB00003B/891